NANNIES

NANNIES

How I Went Through Eighteen Nannies
for One Little Boy Before I Found
Perfection in a Former Marine Sergeant
Named Margaret

Elizabeth Fuller

DONALD I. FINE, INC.
New York

Library of Congress Cataloging-in-Publication Data

Fuller, Elizabeth,
    Nannies : how I went through eighteen nannies for one little boy before I found perfection in a former Marine sergeant named Margaret / Elizabeth Fuller.
        p.   cm.
    ISBN 1-55611-349-8
    1. Nannies—United States—Case studies.   I. Title.
HQ778.7.U6F83   1993
649'.1—dc20   92-54465
                                                                   CIP

For my sister Annie

CHAPTER 1

"SERGEANT MARGARET STONE reporting for duty ma'am," said a wiry redhead in her late twenties. The trousers of her crisp combat fatigues were bloused over spit-shined black leather boots as she stood at parade rest on the doorstep of our New England cottage.

"Ma'am, I apologize for bein' six minutes late," she said. "I departed my former duty station at 0700 calculatin' arrival at 1530. I got a flat." She jerked her head toward a 1965 Mustang in mint condition.

"No problem," I said.

I offered to carry one of her two duffle bags up to her room. She politely declined, and instead tossed a bag to Christopher, our eight-year-old son, her new charge, and ordered: "Stow it under my rack, 'Cruit!"

Stunned, he picked up the bag, "My name's *Chris*, not Cruit!"

Margaret ignored him.

"I hope your room doesn't smell too much of fresh paint," I said, leading Margaret up the stairs.

"Yeah," Christopher piped in, "Birgit, my last nanny, wrote fuck in Swedish all over the walls because her boyfriend wouldn't marry her after he knocked her up."

"Christopher!" I snapped.

"That's what I heard Dad telling Mrs. Hollenbeck!"

1

"Sergeant Margaret Stone reporting for duty, Ma'am."

"Enough, Chris!" I said.

Chris shoved Margaret's bag under the twin bed. Then he turned to her and said: "I hope you have a bra in there. Birgit didn't wear one. That caused a lot of problems around here!"

"Chris!" I gasped.

"Cruit," Margaret said, "I'd like to inspect your quarters. She pulled a poster from her bag. "We'll put this on the bulkhead."

The poster depicted a handsome Marine in dress blues. The caption read: THE MARINES ARE LOOKING FOR A FEW GOOD MEN. Christopher looked at the poster skeptically, scrunched up his still chubby cheeks, and asked: "Were you *really* in the Marines?"

"Does Howdy Doody have a wooden ass?" Margaret answered.

When Mrs. Hollenbeck of the Hollenbeck Nanny Agency learned about Birgit, she sent a string of nannies to be interviewed with promises that if we couldn't find a suitable replacement within a month we would get a full refund—minus Birgit's airfare from Stockholm—as clearly stated in the contract.

After interviewing more than a dozen nannies, we hired Margaret. I had had my fill of Swedish bombshells parading around the house in Guess jeans and tank tops two sizes too small, turning my husband into a drooling Swedish meatball each time they entered the room. I had also had my fill of Iowa farm girls who have never been off the prairie instructing me on how to raise my child.

Margaret, on the other hand, was respectful, disciplined, and eager to undo the damage created by previous nannies. There had been eighteen of them to be exact. This may sound like a lot, but according to the International Nanny Association in Austin, Texas, eighteen nannies in eight years was just slightly above average.

I wish I had been armed with this knowledge nine years earlier when my biological clock was ticking away.

Elizabeth Fuller

*   *   *

I was thirty-five years old when my first and only child was born. The moment the obstetrician placed the tiny bundle in my arms, I looked into his deep, unfocused eyes and thought: "Don't worry my precious gift, I'll never make the same mistakes *my* parents made. No Kool-Aid, cartoons and cap pistols for you. *You* have a mother who recognizes that soft music, melodic voices, good literature and repeated exposure to fine art will nurture your growing mind. Just because Mommy works and cannot be with you every moment, you're not going to suffer the consequences. Mommy has hired an English nanny for you. Her name is Beatrice. Beatrice speaks the King's English. Her last position was with Lady Wellington, a royal cousin of somebody or other . . ."

Watching the doctor weigh and measure tiny Christopher, I imagined him as a toddler, darting around the backyard, dressed like Little Lord Fauntleroy, and calling to me with a British accent. I also visualized myself in a lawn chair, wearing a Laura Ashley frock, having high tea while Christopher plucked wildflowers with Beatrice.

Nine weeks after Christopher was born, John and I packed the baby into his carseat and drove to Kennedy Airport to pick up Beatrice who arrived from London via Freddy Laker's Express. Her flight was delayed three hours. Nobody was happy about this, except for Beatrice. During the flight she had made fast friends with a young man named Guy. Guy played lead guitar in a band in New York called The Users. Guy and Beatrice had identical hairdos, various shades of neon spikes, and matching colds.

On the ride back to Connecticut, Beatrice sat in the front seat next to John, alternately sneezing loudly and quizzing him about her days off, and the best way to get to New York.

"Pop, have you a clue how often the double-deckers run into New York?"

"Double-deckers?" John asked, taken aback.

"Transportation, Pop," Beatrice said. She appeared to be terribly amused that John didn't know what double-deckers were.

4

NANNIES

I sat in the back seat beside Chris, attempting to keep Beatrice's hacking cough and wet sneezes out of Chris's face. In scratchy cockney she said: "Mum, I got me a bitch of a cold. I can crash for a fortnight!"

Beatrice would have worked out fine had John and I brought her over to look after a head shop instead of a baby. The day we parted company, I came home unexpectedly to find my six-month-old son bouncing up and down in his Johnny Jump Up, keeping time to the Sex Pistols. His corn-silk hair was spiked and sprayed hot pink and lime green.

The following evening Guy loaded Beatrice and her Sony boombox into his VW van, and they drove off into a punk sunset.

With Beatrice gone, John and I decided not to bring another stranger into the house. We would tackle the job. Fortunately we worked at home. We were writers, not tied down to regular hours. This enabled us to coordinate our schedules so that one of us would be with Christopher at all times.

Our careers did not interfere in any way with our priority: satisfying Christopher's every need. When he so much as whimpered, he was swept up lest he self-destruct if left alone for five seconds. Whenever he chortled, we ran to him. When he made even the slightest gesture of discomfort, we were there. After three weeks, we were exhausted, irritable, and on the phone to the Hollenbeck Nanny Agency.

Mrs. Hollenbeck was quick to inform us that we were calling at the busiest time of the year, and that her fee went up ten percent to cover increases in overhead. Her tone was formal and scolding. But when I reminded her of Beatrice, she softened and said: "I have the most perfect young woman for you. Her name is Holly. I'm sending her over pronto."

Mrs. Hollenbeck was right. Holly was perfect. She was twenty years old, bright, energetic, spoke with the most charming Canadian accent, and was just meaty enough around the middle to not distract John. She even brought along her pet bird, Mr. Unger—a parrot who doubled as a watchdog. Holly had taught him how to growl every time the doorbell rang.

I came home unexpectedly to find my six month old son bounding
up and down in his Johnny Jump Up, keeping time to the Sex
Pistols. Beatrice had spiked his hair and sprayed it hot
pink and lime green.

John and I both agreed that a nanny with a pet would be a great learning experience for Christopher. And best of all, Holly detested heavy metal. Loud music with an anapestic beat made Mr. Unger crazy. Even Ravel's *Bolero* drove him nuts.

There was only one hitch. Holly wouldn't be able to start for a month. She needed to give her present employer time to find a new nanny. John and I felt it was well worth the wait. We admired Holly's sense of loyalty and responsibility.

While we waited for Holly, I began to have second thoughts: Was Holly everything she appeared to be? If Holly was so exceptional a nanny, why was she leaving her present place of employment? Was it *really* because the family she was working for was allergic to her parrot? Or was there something about Holly nobody was saying?

The morning Holly arrived was hectic. Christopher was cutting a tooth, and only wanted to be held. John's editor was coming for lunch, and to review confidential research material that was scattered throughout his office in large cartons. For the first time since Chris was born, I was going to New York to meet a friend for lunch and catch a play.

When I arrived home, a somber John greeted me at the door.

"What's the matter with you?" I asked.

"Liz," John said in a flat, deadly tone. "Mr. Unger crapped all over my confidential research material."

For a brief moment, I thought John was referring to his editor. Then I remembered that Mr. Unger was Holly's parrot.

"Who let him out of his cage?" I asked.

Between clenched teeth John said: "I was told that he has a trick beak. He let himself out!"

"Where're Holly and Christopher now?"

"In her room, escaping my wrath."

"You didn't upset her, did you?"

"Not yet!" John said, disappearing into his office with a wet sponge and a bar of soap.

I went to Holly's room. Mr. Unger was perched on the pillow. My new pillow case looked like a Jackson Pollock painting.

Holly brought along her pet bird, Mr. Unger, a parrot with a trick
beak who doubled as a watch dog.

Christopher was on the floor. He had his hand inside the bird-cage, playing with gummy earth tones on the newspaper.

I quickly plucked Chris off the floor, and thought: "What's wrong with this picture?"

"Mr. Unger has diarrhea," Holly said, stroking his orange and yellow head.

"I'm sorry to hear that. But Mr. Unger cannot fly around the house. Unless you housebreak him."

"We're working on that," Holly said, nuzzling up next to him. "I don't think it'll be too difficult. He's very bright. He knows twelve words and barks."

Mr. Unger's loose bowels cleared up in three days—thanks to Dr. Morgan, the local vet. From what I gathered, Mr. Unger was no stranger to the emergency ward at the pet hospital. He had an extensive medical history that dated back two years, from just about the time Holly arrived in Connecticut.

It was totally by accident that I discovered why Holly needed to give her last employer three weeks' notice. She had to work the extra time to pay them back for footing Mr. Unger's vet bill. I learned about this when Dr. Morgan's secretary asked me to cosign for his latest charge: fecal analysis.

No sooner was Mr. Unger back on his feet than he developed an irregular heartbeat. Dr. Morgan performed a complete workup that included: blood chemistries, blood count with differential, and selected biopsies. When it was all said and done, I was into Dr. Morgan for $475.00.

Three days before Christmas, Holly went home to Edmonton with plans to return on New Year's Day. At the end of January, I received a phone call. She was not coming back. Holly decided that John's "incredibly anal attitude" toward Mr. Unger caused his medical condition, chronic arrhythmia. Holly thought it would be best if she found a home that was "bird-friendly." She did, however, say that she had grown so fond of Christopher and me, that if only John was out of the picture everything would be ideal. I told Holly that for the moment, I was terribly in love with John, but if the situation changed, she'd be the first to know. We parted with me $475.00 in the hole.

*　　*　　*

Eight years and eighteen nannies later, entered Sgt. Margaret
Stone, USMC. She had been the recent victim of a defense
budget cutback, and was still not sold on civilian life. In fact
the military was all Margaret really knew. Her father, two brothers and an uncle were career Marines. She grew up at Camp
Lejeune in North Carolina, and spent her last two years of high
school in Okinawa.

A few days after she was discharged, Margaret packed her
gear into the '65 Mustang and headed north. By the time she
hit Connecticut, she was running low on funds. She saw one
of Mrs. Hollenbeck's ads recruiting nannies in the local paper.
The moment she saw the word "recruit" she felt a new career
looming.

Within days of Margaret's arrival, Christopher was de-
manding that she leave. After having been given free rein by
over a dozen nannies, it now appeared that he was going to
have to, as Margaret so delicately put it, "shape up or ship
out." Since our prime motivation for hiring Margaret was for
education and discipline, Chris's pleas fell on deaf ears. Margaret's background included a "billet" teaching tactics to the new
recruits. Although I hadn't a clue what that was, it sounded
like something that would be good for Chris.

The first month Margaret was with us, I was on a first-name
basis with the UPS delivery man. She ordered every *Time/Life*
war book series advertised on TV. Unlike Holly, Margaret's
credit was good.

Where previous nannies were sloppy, Margaret was meticu-
lous. The sinks shone. Christopher was squeaky-clean. His
clothes had a military press. And he was never bored. He and
Margaret shared the same thirst for blood and heavy artillery.

When Margaret and Christopher weren't charging up from
our river shouting "Die, you gooks!" or "Burn, you Krauts!"
she was organizing field maneuvers with toy soldiers in Chris's
old sandbox, or assaults on Pork Chop Hill—our back deck. Of
course this was after his homework and duties of the day were
completed.

She didn't take any guff from Christopher either. "Cruit,"

she'd say, "if your room isn't cleaned up, you'd better give your soul to God because your ass is mine!"

Margaret set up a chain of command. Chris wasn't encouraged to talk directly to John or me between our working hours of 0800 and 1700. John was the C.O.—commanding officer; I was the X.O—executive officer; and Margaret was the Master Sergeant who ran the day-to-day show. When John or I spoke, she practically saluted, but when Margaret was talking to her peers, other nannies in the neighborhood, I'd hear her say: "Fuckin' A." I gathered that was Marine talk for "yes."

After a month with Margaret, Chris was speaking like a Marine veteran:

"Cruit," Margaret commanded, "eat your chow!"

"I don't have to!"

"That's a direct order!"

"You can't make me eat," Chris protested.

"Cruit, I'll court-martial your ass!"

"I'm going to tell my mother!"

"Cruit, you don't eat that chow, and you'll be standing tall in front of the C.O. He'll slam your ass in the stockade and you'll be eating bread and water. You read me?"

Christopher gave in: "Fuckin' A."

After overhearing that dialogue, I had a chat with Margaret. I told her that although I felt she was doing a splendid job, John and I wanted her to relax the military jargon a tad, and cut back on some of the bloodier maneuvers. I explained that John was a Quaker, and Quakers were opposed to war. I told her that John wouldn't even allow a squirt gun in the house. Margaret looked puzzled, but she accepted our decision as if it had come from the Pentagon.

In the days that followed, however, Margaret reverted back to her old ways. According to Chris she was planning to re-create the assault on Iwo Jima the next time they went to the beach. John and I decided that since Margaret and Chris seemed to be bonding, and Chris's behavior was steadily improving, we'd overlook her somewhat less than intellectual approach to life.

John, however, did not come to this decision easily. I had to

Ozone Joan, the environmentalist, was caught dismantling aerosol cans in the grocery store and slipping the white button caps into Chris's backpack.

remind him of Nanny Number Ten: Ozone Joan, the environmentalist.

Joan came to us highly recommended by Mrs. Hollenbeck. All Mrs. Hollenbeck could tell me about her was that for the previous two years she worked in a mine in the Badlands.

During Joan's first week at our house, she was cornered by an "Ozone Activist" going door-to-door, alerting people to the dangers of aerosol cans. After Joan went to a few local meetings, and devoured the literature, she was reluctant to leave the protective covering of the house. She made herself a Mylar umbrella. Joan's only mission was to go to drugstores and grocery stores to dismantle aerosol cans. I found this out when the manager at Walgreen's phoned to tell me that Joan and Chris were being held in his office. Joan had been caught slipping twelve white button caps into Chris's backpack.

Chris later told me that Joan had been doing that for months, using Chris as the lookout. She told him that if he squealed, she'd pack him off to live with the pygmies in the Amazon rain forest.

When John and I didn't applaud Joan for the Walgreen caper, she called Mrs. Hollenbeck and told her that she couldn't work for a couple who were so insensitive to the environment. Joan left with all my plastic trash bags and styrofoam cups stuffed into a tote bag emblazened with "Save the Earth."

After I reminded John of Ozone Joan, he took a long, thoughtful drag on his pipe and said: "I hope we didn't offend Margaret. She's doing a helluva job with that little monkey."

CHAPTER 2

WHILE I WAS preparing the house for Christmas, Margaret and Christopher were preparing to commemorate the attack on Pearl Harbor. They were hanging flags, I was hanging mistletoe.

Unlike years past, Chris was not preoccupied with Santa Claus and Rudolph, instead he kept his eyes on the horizon, looking for an impending Japanese invasion. With Margaret's binoculars, he spent his free time searching the sky for signs of the red zero.

"Sarge," Christopher called from his bedroom window, "Bogie at twelve o'clock."

Without even bothering to look out the window, Margaret called back, "It's a chopper from the Sikorsky plant, Cruit. But good work and keep your eyes peeled."

I was never quite sure if Margaret was serious or if she was just entertaining Chris.

On the morning of December 7, Margaret sat at the breakfast table sketching a topographical map of the island of Oahu on a napkin, showing Chris the attack route. John sat mute, reading the New York *Times*, trying to pretend that he didn't hear the dialogue.

"Sarge," Chris said, "When the battleships got hit and exploded, were there bodies flying everywhere?"

"Bingo," Margaret said. "Two thousand two hundred and

eighty casualties. F–4Us were dropping out of the sky like turds out of Mr. Unger."

Chris cracked up. He loved hearing stories about Nanny Number Two, and how upset his dad was over the parrot's sloppy little gifts all over his research material. Apparently Chris had shared those stories with Margaret.

"Chris," I said, in an attempt to change the subject, "I bet Margaret would like to go to the pancake breakfast with us on Sunday. Santa Claus will be there."

Margaret didn't look up from the napkin. She was busy drawing the U.S.S. *Arizona* for Chris.

"Are there petrified bodies in there?" Christopher wanted to know.

"Cruit, on December 8, those bodies were nothing but fish food."

John dropped his glasses to the tip of his nose and peered over his paper at me, as if I were responsible for the conversation.

I shrugged my shoulders and poured myself another cup of coffee. I didn't like the conversation anymore than John did, but I felt as if I had a handle on the larger picture. For example, Christopher was learning history. During the last parent/teacher conference, Mrs. Johnson told me that Chris was the only one in social studies who knew where Guam was and that it was best known as a major military base. His teacher also said that since Birgit left, Christopher had much more self-control. He no longer cursed in Swedish during spelling tests.

As far as I was concerned Margaret was doing her job. So what if she had a military bent? It was ingrained in every corpuscle of her being. She couldn't change even if she wanted to. A few days earlier Margaret received a video tape from her father in Okinawa. It was a Christmas message. Margaret invited me to watch it. The tape opened with her father standing at parade rest. His jaw was square and his hair was cropped so close to his head, he might have been bald. Chevrons ran from his shoulder to his wrist.

The message was simple and to the point: TO MY DAUGHTER,

"Jeopardy" was the highlight of Darlene's day. She had the uncanny ability to simulate the sound of the "Jeopardy" buzzer. By the time he was sixteen months old, Chris was simulating it too.

NANNIES

SERGEANT STONE: A VERY MERRY CHRISTMAS AND A HAPPY NEW YEAR. LOVE, MASTER SERGEANT STONE.

The Christmas cheer was followed by a John Wayne movie: *The Sands of Iwo Jima*.

Margaret was tickled with the video. The day it arrived she had a few of the nannies in the neighborhood over for pizza and beer and to see the tape.

It never failed to amaze me how quickly nannies could scout out other nannies in the neighborhood. On our road alone there were four, all from the Midwest. One of them had worked for us. Her name was Darlene. She was an idiot savant.

Darlene was a twenty-two-year-old girl from Nebraska, and a leading authority on absolutely everything, except childcare. "Jeopardy!" was the high point of her day. Darlene could rattle off the population of every city in the U.S., but she couldn't remember to feed Chris his lunch or change his diaper. She had the uncanny ability to simulate the sound of the "Jeopardy!" buzzer while at the same time pantomiming the joystick. One evening I threw a Stump-the-Nanny party. John thought he had her with: "The greatest of the early Greek poets."

Darlene made the customary guttural noise, and barked: "Who was Sappho?"

"Wrong!" John exclaimed triumphantly. "It was Homer!"

We checked. Darlene was correct. The game continued until I finally got her with: "A place to put dirty dishes."

First came the noise, then the answer: "What's a landfill?"

When Christopher turned sixteen months and was regularly simulating the "Jeopardy!" buzzer, I had a talk with Darlene. I told her in no uncertain terms that it was critical that Chris hear *human* words so that he could begin to build a vocabulary. Darlene ignored me. She continued to watch and even tape "Jeopardy!" Sometimes she had two TV sets going at the same time. John became involved the morning he overheard Chris screeching his lungs out in front of the TV.

"Christ!" John roared, as he darted out of his office into the family room, "what the *hell* is going on?"

John found Chris hanging over the top of the playpen slap-

17

ping the palm of his hand on the TV table, pantomiming the "Jeopardy!" buzzer. On one of the slaps, he caught his hand on the edge of the metal TV carousel. It was swollen and bruised.

While John put ice on Chris's tiny hand, he laid down the law: "No more 'Jeopardy!'"

That evening Darlene told us that it was critical that she follow her bliss. Two weeks later she was on the redeye to L.A., committed to making it as a contestant on game shows.

Six weeks later she was back. Although we had already hired a new nanny, we let her stay with us until she found another job. Within days she was hired to take care of the baby down the road after their Norwegian nanny split with husband Howard and the new Volvo.

Everybody saw it coming, except for wife Janet whose mind was on teaching their infant math and Japanese with flash cards. I felt she pushed Jason into academics because he was forced to drop out of Water Babies. He kept mistaking the pool's fresh water supply nozzle for his mother's breast.

There was no doubt about it, Janet was ridiculous with those flash cards. She always made me feel guilty for denying Chris the gift of bilingualism. Nevertheless my heart went out to her. She deserved better. While poor Janet was doing flash cards, Howard was doing Elsa.

Four years later, Howard was back with Janet. They had another child, Page. The last time I bumped into Janet, she told me, "Page is so eclectic. She adores lunching at Celestial Seasonings. She *craves* the tahini lemon sauce smeared on her zwieback." I thought to myself: Howard's a pretty eclectic guy too. I wonder what he "craves" smeared on his zwieback?

Actually, I saw more of Howard than I did of Janet. I often bumped into him early in the morning when Chris and I were waiting for the schoolbus. He would jog by on the way to his orthodontics office with five-pound weights strapped to his ankles. He had a perpetual half-smile on his face, sort of like the Pope. It seemed to say: I've got a secret, and I'm not telling.

Sometimes Margaret and I would both wait with Chris at the bus stop. Margaret called Howard a pussywimp under her breath as he ran by. Since Margaret and Darlene were good friends, Margaret knew the entire saga of Howard and Janet and former nanny Elsa.

I once asked Margaret if she thought Howard was still messing around. Margaret pretended that she didn't hear me. She was very tight-lipped when it came to gossip. But a few days later, I overheard her in the family room talking to Darlene about Howard:

"That's the last time that maggot's going to play grabass with my butt!" Margaret said.

Darlene asked, "Did you really deck him?"

Margaret responded: "Fuckin' A."

Although Margaret wasn't particularly pretty, she was attractive. I thought if she would let her short-cropped hair grow, take off the wire rims, and wear a little makeup, she'd be quite attractive. One day I gave Margaret mascara and eye shadow to bring out her almond-shaped green eyes. Margaret used it as camouflage paint during a re-creation of a field exercise with Chris.

With the holidays over, we were all looking forward to some rest. Margaret had knocked herself out making sure that Christopher had a great Christmas.

Margaret's mother split from her father when she was only six years old, leaving him with Margaret and her two brothers. "I never got an Easter basket, a quarter under my pillow, or a Valentine," Margaret said. Her eyes told the whole story.

Since Margaret didn't go home for the holidays, we gave her a rather nice-sized Christmas bonus. We knew that she needed to save up for her visit to Okinawa. Her brother was getting married in the spring. But instead of saving the money, she must have spent every penny on gifts for us. We were embarrassed but deeply touched by her generosity. John even overlooked the Uzi machine gun and camouflage gear for Chris.

By the end of February we had all recuperated from the Christmas hoopla, and were in the process of planning a ski week in Vermont.

"Mom," Chris said, "Sarge doesn't know how to ski, and I'm

going to teach her. And she's going to teach me all about cold weather survival."

"What's cold weather survival?" I asked.

"You know, Mom, it's surviving in the elements using only your instincts, and what nature has to offer."

For the next week, every time I looked out the kitchen window, I saw Chris and a handful of neighborhood kids, ankle deep in snow, marching to cadence in the backyard. Margaret was alongside, making certain nobody broke step.

KIDS: Our troop leader chews on nails,
She will kick our little tails
Sound off—one, two

MARGARET: If you little maggots squeal,
I've got a fist that's hard as steel!
Sound off—three, four

CHORUS: One, two, three, four
One, two—three, four

Two days before our ski trip, Margaret received a telegram. Her father had suffered a massive heart attack and was in intensive care at the base hospital.

Distraught, Margaret packed her bags. The next day we drove her to the airport where she boarded Japan Airlines for Okinawa. We told Margaret to stay with her father as long as she was needed. Somehow we would manage without her. She clicked her heels together and disappeared into the jetway.

Ten days after Margaret left, she sent a telegram: TO MR. AND MRS. FULLER. STOP. DAD'S STILL IN INTENSIVE CARE. STOP. PROGNOSIS LOOKING BETTER. STOP. WILL WRITE MORE LATER. STOP.

Margaret added a special message for Christopher: CRUIT, HOPE SKI MOBILIZATION EXERCISE ON MT. SNOW WENT AS PLANNED. STOP. LOVE, SARGE.

During Margaret's absence, Mrs. Hollenbeck sent us a temporary nanny. A lovely, mature woman from Alabama. That was my impression. Chris had his own.

"Mom, Mrs. Kibble's crazy!"

"Christopher," I said, "she's a perfectly lovely lady. Don't you just love her deep-dish apple pie?"

"Mom, she told me that she's working for the CIA, and that if I didn't take down my Marine poster she'd report me to Langley, Virginia. She talks to herself in a weird, scary voice!"

Mrs. Kibble had the most lyrical voice. I was sure that Chris's imagination had been fertilized by Margaret.

"Mrs. Kibble is very fond of you, Chris. She'd be deeply hurt if she heard you now."

"Mom, I promise you, she told me that she was a double agent, and if I did one little thing to piss her off, I'd be dog meat!"

"I don't like that language, Christopher!"

"I'm just telling you what she said to me. She even uses the "F" word when she's talking to herself!"

"Enough, Chris!" I said, ending all further discussion about sweet Mrs. Kibble.

That evening I found a postcard on Chris's desk, earmarked for Okinawa. "Dear Sarge," he wrote, "Hurry back. There's a real crazy taking care of me. I miss you. Love, Cruit."

Several days later, the phone rang. It was a secretary at the Russian embassy. A woman with a heavy, but precise Russian accent asked to speak to Mrs. Marian Kibble. I told her that she was out, and asked if there was a message.

"Yes," the woman said, "Mrs. Kibble has been sending us résumés and duplicated blueprints from *Mechanics Illustrated*. We want her to stop contacting the embassy at once."

Aghast, I hung up the phone. Christopher was right. Mrs. Kibble was one melon ball short of a fruit cup. I went into her bedroom. On the dresser was a copy of *The Falcon and the Snowman: A True Story of Friendship and Espionage*. Next to the book was a bottle of pills.

I called Mrs. Hollenbeck and demanded that she tell me *everything* she knew about Mrs. Kibble.

Mrs. Hollenbeck became defensive. "Mrs. Fuller, I run a top-notch agency. All my nannies are screened with the closest of scrutiny . . ."

I cut her off. "What about Mary from the Philippines. How'd she slip through?"

Mrs. Hollenbeck became so quiet, I could hear her asthmatic Pekinese wheezing on the other end of the line.

Mary was Nanny Number Four. John dubbed her "The Philippine Philanthropist." Mary had a curious habit of giving away my household items. Once a week, I'd notice a large box leaving my house addressed to Manila. The moment I came home from the A&P, Mary would take the empty brown paper bags, string, and packaging tape to her room.

One time I questioned her about the contents of a heavy box that rattled, and had FRAGILE printed on all sides. She said it was popcorn.

In the four months Mary was with us only one package arrived. It arrived after she had already left. It contained my coffee grinder. Evidently it didn't work on 220 current.

Mary's replacement was Wendy. In Hollenbeck's words: "Wendy is a Class A nanny." This was true. Wendy was a Class A nanny on warm, dry days. But on days with high humidity she became unpredictable, exhibiting amnesia. Twice, during a drizzling rain, she had driven to the corner market and walked home. No car. No groceries. The first time that happened, I called the police and reported my car as missing. We ended up having to ground Wendy on humid, sticky days.

Just when we were at our wits' end, we'd have a spell of dry sunny weather, and couldn't imagine our lives without Wendy. Then one day while we were going on our annual visit to my parents in Cleveland, Wendy set off the metal detector at the airport. She had a metal plate in her head that caused her eccentric behavior.

I had no time to argue with Mrs. Hollenbeck over her tight

screening process. Simply, she knew absolutely *nothing* about Mrs. Kibble's past, just as she had known *nothing* about Mary's and Wendy's.

I hung up, grabbed Mrs. Kibble's bottle of pills and tried to read the label. Someone had scratched out the name of the prescription. In the right-hand corner was the name of a doctor. Underneath his name was a telephone number with a 223 Area Code. I looked in the phone book. It was Montgomery, Alabama. Of course, I thought, that's where Mrs. Kibble's from.

Earlier in the day, Mrs. Kibble was telling me about the blue ribbon she won for her deep-dish apple pie in Montgomery's annual Betty Crocker Bake-Off.

I picked up the phone and dialed the number.

"Mrs. Fuller," said the doctor in a slow, easy, Southern drawl, "I know good help is hard to find, but I wouldn't want my child being looked after by a woman with Mrs. Kibble's medical condition."

"Doctor, what exactly *is* Mrs. Kibble's medical condition?"

"I suppose I shouldn't be discussing this with a stranger, but as a daddy of three, I sure don't want to see anything happen to your young son." There was a brief pause. Then he said: "Mrs. Fuller, you got yourself a paranoid schizophrenic living in your house."

My first reaction was no reaction. There must be some sort of logical explanation for all of this. My second reaction, however, turned me into an hysterical mother who just learned that her only child was out somewhere with a paranoid schizophrenic who spent her leisure time sending blueprints from *Mechanics Illustrated* to the Russian embassy.

I collected my thoughts. Then I went to John's office and shared the news flash.

"Don't panic," I said, weaving around a few boxes of research. My voice was quivering. "I just learned that Mrs. Kibble's a paranoid schizophrenic."

"Yeah?" John said. His head was buried in a textbook about tornadoes. I was sure he hadn't taken in a word I'd said.

"This is no joke!" I said. I told him all about the phone call to the Southern doctor, and that Christopher and Mrs. Kibble were out somewhere.

John looked like a startled fawn caught in the headlights of an oncoming car.

"Liz," John said, with his hand on the phone, "I'm calling the state police."

"No!" I grabbed the receiver out of his hand. "She's dangerous. If she spots police, there's no telling what she'll do."

"Where do you think they are?" John asked.

"They could be anywhere!"

"I'm going out to look for them," John said. He dropped his pipe in the ashtray and flicked off his computer all in one move.

"I'll wait here," I said.

While I stood at the window, watching for Mrs. Kibble's dark green Chevy, I was haunted by what Chris had told me at the breakfast table, only hours earlier.

"Mom, when Mrs. Kibble drives me to soccer practice, she closes her eyes so she can see how far she can go before she crashes headlong into somebody. It's really scary, and you don't care! Wait till I tell Sarge. She'll believe me!"

My response was: "Christopher, finish your homework."

Just as I picked up the phone to call the police, Mrs. Kibble pulled into the driveway.

Christopher leaped out of the car, toting a McDonald's kid meal pack, mumbling under his breath, "She almost killed me this time, Mom."

I hugged Chris as if I hadn't seen him for a lifetime. Then I turned to Mrs. Kibble, who had the most beatific smile on her face, and said that we needed to talk in private. I took her upstairs to my office.

As I closed the door, I had no idea what I was going to say to her. Suddenly, in a flash, I had devised a plan. I would fight fire with fire or, in this case, craziness with craziness.

I went to my desk drawer where I had some money stashed, and slipped it into an envelope.

"Mrs. Kibble," I whispered, "take this money. While you

Mrs. Kibble was a lovely, mature woman from Alabama who baked wonderful cookies when she wasn't sending blueprints from *Mechanics Illustrated* to the Russian Embassy.

were out, the CIA was here looking for you. They're planning on staking out the house tonight. There's enough money in that envelope to get you back to Montgomery. Go to your family. They'll hide you. If you hurry you can escape before they return."

Mrs. Kibble's cherubic face turned to that of a crazed fugitive on the run.

"How much do they know?" she asked, barely audible.

"Everything," I said in a breathy voice. "Now you must go quickly. And never come back. Do you understand?"

Mrs. Kibble nodded her well coiffed gray head, as if we were coconspirators. In less than ten minutes she was packed and on the run.

CHAPTER 3

ON THE FIRST DAY of Spring, we received another telegram from Margaret. TO MR. AND MRS. FULLER. STOP. DAD'S RELEASED FROM HOSPITAL AND ON MEND. STOP. REQUEST PERMISSION TO STAY FOR BROTHER'S WEDDING. STOP. IF ACCEPTABLE, WILL RETURN STATESIDE APRIL 12. STOP.

As in all of Margaret's telegrams she added a special message for Chris.

CRUIT, I'LL BE BACK IN PLENTY OF TIME FOR YOUR BIRTHDAY. STOP. LOVE, SARGE

We wired her back: TO SERGEANT MARGARET STONE. STOP. THRILLED YOUR DAD'S DOING SO WELL. STOP. HAVE A GLASS OF CHAMPAGNE FOR US AT BROTHER'S WEDDING. STOP.

Chris insisted on sending his own message: SARGE. STOP. BIBBY'S FARM STORIES ARE GROSSING ME OUT. STOP. HURRY BACK. STOP. LOVE, CRUIT.

Bibby moved in two weeks after Mrs. Kibble headed south. Incidentally, a few days after Mrs. Kibble left, I phoned her doctor to see if he knew if she had made it safely back to Montgomery. Fortunately she had. In fact he said that she had landed at her sister's house, spent a couple of days there, locked in the guest room with all the shades pulled, and now she was resting comfortably in a foam rubber lodge connected to a lovely country hospital, only blocks from her sister's house. She'd been given kitchen privileges in return for her car keys.

Bibby came to us through Mrs. Hollenbeck's rival agency: The Loving Hand. When the agency owner, Mr. Pitkin, learned of my last experience he chuckled and said: "That type of thing will *never* happen with The Loving Hand. Even our temporary nannies have had their police and motor vehicle records checked."

Then Mr. Pitkin told me that it was my lucky day. "I have a gem for you," he said. "And she's willing to work as a temp."

He told me that her name was Bibby. She was a twenty-year-old girl, born and bred on an Ohio dairy farm. She was in *Who's Who in 4-H*, the talented and gifted program in high school, and she taught Bible study to youngsters. He gave me a list of references, and her telephone number.

"Can you want for anything more?" Mr. Pitkin asked.

"Yes," I said. "I'd like to meet her."

"I'm afraid that's not possible," Mr. Pitkin said. "Unless, of course, you're planning a trip to Twinsburg in the next few days."

He pulled her photograph out of a file. It was a high-school headshot of a plump but pleasant-looking girl.

"Well," I said, studying the photo, "I'm *definitely* going to check her references."

"Please do," he said, "You'll find they're impeccable. And she has a twin sister, Barby, who just happens to be a nanny for a family right in your neighborhood."

"Can I phone the family?"

"If you'd let me finish, that's exactly what I was getting at."

The family's praise for Bibby's sister sent me scurrying back to The Loving Hand where I signed a contract, and forked over a check.

Four days later, a Honda Civic lumbered into our driveway, hauling Bibby and Barby.

The twins rolled out of the car, each carrying the remains of a jumbo Dairy Queen.

"Oh, my God!" Chris cried, as these rosy-cheeked girls in T-shirts that said "Twinsburg is for lovers" ambled toward the house. "Hulk Hogan and Jake-the-Snake!"

Once in the house, I began to explain to Bibby what her chores would involve, Chris sat mute, snuggled next to his dad. His eyes were bugged half out of his head.

"You'll need to drive Chris to soccer practice twice a week," I said, adding, "You do know how to drive a stick shift?"

"Sure I can drive a stick shift," Bibby said. "But only if it's a tractor."

"Dad," Chris whispered, "are we going to get a tractor?"

John cleared his throat and left the room.

I excused myself and followed him to his office.

"Listen," I said, "this is going to be a *great* learning experience for Christopher."

"The luckmeister is with us" John jeered.

"Do you realize that Chris has never even been to a farm? All he knows are the suburbs and city. What does that say about us?"

"Liz, have you ever spent time on a farm?"

"As a matter of fact when I was a kid, every Sunday my father packed us into the 1955 Buick, and we drove out into the country. Sometimes we'd buy fresh corn or pumpkins or tomatoes out of the back of a farmer's pickup truck. The farmers were always so friendly. I loved the smell of the country. It always smelled like fresh-cut grass. My mother would call out every few minutes, "Look at the cows!" I have to admit that after about the first half-hour my brother and I would be in the back seat beating each other up. My father would be flailing his right arm into the back seat, threatening to pull off the side of the road and smack us. Then my mother would draw an imaginary line between Gary and me . . ."

"And the one who crossed over the line got dumped in a cornfield," John interrupted.

"How'd you know?"

"Remember, I had three yard apes before Chris," John said.

Because John's kids were grown, I would sometimes forget that he had had a whole life before me. I first met John at 35,000 feet. I was a flight attendant and he was a passenger. I'll never forget our first words to each other. "Excuse me, sir," I said,

29

"are you the writer?" And he looked up from his book and said, "Are you the stewardess?"

I should have known then that John could slice through hours of conversation with a few well-chosen words.

Now, on the way out of John's office, he did not disappoint me. "Liz," he said, tossing me the Yellow Pages, "look up a John Deere store."

"Very funny," I said. "You'll see, she's going to be very good for Chris."

That evening at dinner I said to Bibby, "Tell Chris what it's like to grow up on a real dairy farm."

John piped in, "Bibby, I want to know why there's an expiration date on sour cream."

Bibby looked genuinely puzzled.

"John's just teasing," I said.

"How many cows do you have?" Chris asked.

"That's a very good question," I said, proud of Chris's curiosity.

Bibby helped herself to a couple of chicken legs and said, "Two less than we had in the winter."

"Oh," I said.

"This past spring, I was on the combine," Bibby began, "when I noticed that two of our heifers got outside the fence and were in quicksand."

Chris interrupted: "There's no such thing as quicksand!"

"There sure is!" Bibby said. "These two heifers were sinking faster than the *Titanic.*"

"How'd you get them out?" I asked, confident of a folksy ending.

"Pa and I rigged up the tractor and tried hauling them out. By this time the heifers were sinking fast—up to their necks, then noses, then eyeballs . . ."

"Stop!" Chris screeched.

John sat alarmingly silent.

Bibby turned to Chris and said, "Son, if you ever get trapped in quicksand, just stay as still as possible and you'll have an extra few minutes to do your final reckoning with the Big Man upstairs."

When Bibby got up to get Chris another glass of milk, I whispered to John, "Don't worry, I know this story has a happy ending."

"Yeah," John hissed, "It ended up as USDA prime rib at the dinner table."

"Bibby," I said, certain that there must be an Old Mac-Donald ending, "what finally happened?"

Bibby picked a chicken wing clean and said, "They just sank out of sight."

Bibby stayed with us until Margaret returned. During that time we learned more about life on a farm than we cared to know. We learned that a single cow produces twelve tons of manure a year. The chicken that you kill yourself doesn't taste as good as the kind you buy from Frank Perdue. If a pig is out of his pen, he is twice as smart as the people trying to corral him. Pigs have a great sense of family and humor. A turkey can drown by staring at the sky during a thunderstorm. Cow pies don't taste good. Chickens don't have lips. The blunt end of an egg comes out first. Cows have the same menstrual cycle as women. Some have P.M.S. Billy goats smell worse than skunks. When you shoot a steer it can sometimes fall on top of you.

On the morning of Margaret's arrival, Chris decorated the house with balloons and crepe paper. On his computer, he printed out a large banner for over the fireplace: WELCOME HOME SARGE. WE REALLY MISSED YOU!

I made a cake and Christopher decorated it with tiny plastic soldiers. Instead of flowers, Christopher squeezed miniature hand grenades out of the frosting tube. I drew the line when he wanted to splatter red dye over a few of the soldiers.

At seven o'clock, John and Christopher went to the airport to pick up Margaret. While they were gone, several of Margaret's nanny friends came over as a special surprise. Even Howard showed up. He said that Janet was at a week-long refresher course at the Better Baby Institute, the flash card place, and he thought it would be fun to welcome Margaret home. He couldn't stay though. He had to cram for his lingual appliance certification. But he certainly could have a bite of cake and ice cream.

When we heard John tap his horn three times, we all darted into the back bedroom. The moment the front door opened and Chris called: "Gee, I guess Mom must be out!" we ran out of the room to greet Margaret.

I later discovered that we didn't all run out to greet Margaret. Howard and Gretchen—a buxom German girl—stayed behind to have their "cake and ice cream" on the Castro Convertible.

At the end of the evening, Margaret accidently walked in on the naked tooth doctor and his Fräulein.

Livid, Margaret plucked up Howard's jeans and ordered: "Pussywimp, hit the deck and give me fifty!"

The commotion caused by Margaret's order drew everyone's attention. The first person through the door was Darlene.

"Dr. Martin!" gasped Darlene—the "Jeopardy!" Queen— "what is infidelity?"

"Darlene," Howard said, frantically looking for something to cover himself, "this isn't what it appears."

"What are two naked people on a Castro Convertible?" Darlene demanded.

"I can explain," Howard said.

"Explain it to your wife!" Darlene snapped.

I could see the blood drain from Howard's face—and other extremeties.

Yes, it was good to have Margaret back and order restored. That night, Christopher fell asleep on Margaret's shoulder while she read aloud from *The Assault on Guadalcanal*.

CHAPTER 4

THREE DAYS AFTER Margaret's welcome-home party, Howard's wife appeared at my door. Her Giorgio Armani shades couldn't hide the torment in her eyes. I was sure that Darlene had spilled out the whole ugly story, just as she had promised. John had been sitting in the kitchen finishing his breakfast.

"Liz," John whispered, "just don't get involved!"

"So how'd it go at the Better Baby Institute?" I asked, avoiding all discussion of Casanova on the Castro.

Janet flipped the sunglasses to the top of her head and poured her heart out: "Page was *très impossible*. During oral testing, she *refused* to speak even one word of her second language. And when I held up her favorite Cezanne card, she grabbed it, shoved it in her mouth, and then spit up all over Monet's *Terrace at Le Havre*, also a favorite."

John winced and left the room.

I looked over at Margaret. She was at the stove making S.O.S., marine talk for creamed chipped beef on toast, for Christopher and herself. The entire time Janet spoke Margaret shook her head in disbelief.

Janet nibbled a wrapped nail and droned on: "The last day of the workshop, Page got a miserable cold. Her cold medication made her so tired she nodded in and out of sleep. Finally, I got her awake long enough to count to three in Japanese—her third language. But I'm not at all certain that she actually said, "ichi, ni, san," or if she was making a "do-do . . ."

"Excuse me, ma'am," Margaret interrupted, "you requested that I remind you of your conference call at ten hundred—that's in five minutes," Margaret winked.

"Thanks, Margaret." I returned the wink.

As Janet got up to leave, she reached into her Louis Vuitton handbag and said, "Oh, Margaret, I found this T-shirt on the floor of Howard's car. It's not Darlene's. It must be yours."

Margaret inspected the crumpled T-shirt. Across the chest were bold German letters: ICH ZAHLE MIT PLASTIK UND LIEBE MIT LATEX.

Translated: I pay with plastic and love with latex. Howard and Gretchen had had it printed at the mall.

Janet asked the snickering Margaret what it meant.

Margaret clammed up.

Janet asked again.

"Ma'am," Margaret said, "I suggest you ask Page."

Janet, not dialed into the dig, said, "Page isn't due to study German until she's two."

Then a sudden look of panic flashed across Janet's face—her woman's intuition apparently kicked into high gear. "This shirt does belong to you?" Janet asked in a shaky, high-pitched voice.

Margaret and Janet were eyeball to eyeball.

I was sure that Margaret was going to sing. I didn't want to be a part of this. I thought back five years to the time when Howard, Elsa and the Volvo were on a slow boat to Martha's Vineyard, and Janet was on the phone to the police naively reporting the three as missing. Janet and the two kids had come home four days early from visiting the grandparents in Boca Raton.

The local police, who got their training watching "Mayberry" reruns, dusted the whole house for fingerprints from top to bottom. After the entire passive-solar contemporary was roped off with yellow tape that read: POLICE BARRICADE DO NOT PASS, the police chief figured out that it wasn't the butler who did it in the green room with a knife. It was Howard who did it in the nanny's room with his poker.

When the police spelled it out to Janet, she went into shock. Then she went into Howard's office and smashed all of his plaster dental molds to a fine powder.

I was thinking about all of this when Margaret snapped the T-shirt out of Janet's hand and said, "Yes, it's mine."

There was marked relief on Janet's face. There was marked compassion on Margaret's.

As the Volvo wagon pulled out of our driveway and onto the narrow country road, I said: "Margaret, that T-shirt belongs to Gretchen, doesn't it?"

"Bingo!" Margaret said.

"I thought for sure that you were going to say something."

Margaret tucked her camouflage shirt into her trousers and said, "Ma'am, my father brought me up to never pass up an opportunity to keep my mouth shut."

I went to sleep that night with a sense of wonderment and reverence for Margaret. It took eighteen nannies to get to her. I vowed never to take her for granted.

As I drifted off to sleep thoughts of Ginger, Nanny Number Seven, floated in and out of my mind.

Ginger was a twenty-year-old from Minnesota. She answered an ad I put in the local paper: WORKING COUPLE SEEKING A BRIGHT, ENERGETIC YOUNG WOMAN WHO WOULD LOVE TO LOOK AFTER A VERY ACTIVE SIX-YEAR-OLD BOY.

The following week Ginger moved in. What I didn't know at the time was that Ginger had P.M.S. so bad that it knocked her out of commission twenty-two days a month. The week of her period she suffered migraines and cramps that landed her in bed. The week after was recovery time. The third week Ginger was Nanny of the Year. The week before her period she had violent mood swings. She was bloated, depressed, and anxious about getting her period, or in her words: Riding the cotton pony.

I found myself scheduling Christopher's sixth birthday party around Ginger's menstrual cycle. The closest we could come was three weeks away. Ginger put a calendar next to mine so that our social life would revolve around her P.M.S.

John and I kept hoping that she'd get pregnant. But there was no chance of that. She spent her free time researching every new over-the-counter medication for P.M.S. and combing pharmacies for the latest improved tampons and Kotex—mini, maxi, light days, etc. She had them all stashed in her closet. I was soon to learn that the feminine products had more than one use.

The second week Ginger was with us, I got a call from Christopher's first-grade teacher. Mrs. Leber's singsong voice metamorphosed into a scolding rasp.

"Mrs. Fuller, Christopher has brought in a most inappropriate art project for 'Winter Scene Week.'"

Before I could ask what it was, she told me.

"Your son has made Santa Claus's workshop out of Kotex and tampons, instead of cotton balls and Q-tips."

"There must be some mistake," I said. "I sent Ginger to buy a whole bag of cotton balls and Q-tips.

"There is no mistake," Mrs. Leber barked. "The tampon strings are reindeer reins, and the plastic applicators are stick figures of Mr. and Mrs. Claus."

"That's absolutely disgusting," I said to the unhinged teacher. "I shall speak sharply to Ginger!"

I hung up the phone and went to Ginger's room. She was flopped on the bed with a thermometer sticking out of her mouth reading a pink pamphlet titled: "Does Your Maxi Pad Continue to Let You Down?"

"Ginger," I said, "why on earth did you make Christopher's 'Winter Scene' project out of Kotex and tampons?"

Ginger burst out crying. In between the sobs, she explained how she had used the cotton ball and Q-tip money for the new basal thermometer that detects the *exact* day of ovulation.

The next conversation I had with Mrs. Leber was about a month later.

She phoned to tell me that Christopher fell asleep at his desk during story time. And when she asked him if he were feeling well, he snapped, "No!"

"Can you tell me how you feel?" Mrs. Leber asked.

"Anxious, bloated, depressed," he grumbled. He ran his fingers through his Dutch boy haircut and asked, "Do you have any Midol?"

With every passing month, John's concern grew that Christopher would grow up to be the first teenage boy to suffer P.M.S. Then eight months after Ginger moved in, she came to us and said that she just learned that the Mayo Clinic in Rochester, Minnesota—five miles from her parents' home—was looking for volunteers to participate in a study to evaluate a new product for P.M.S. Ginger left with our blessing and a fresh supply of Midol.

The day Ginger left, I did some heavy-duty self-analysis. What was it within me that allowed for Ginger and all of her predecessors to take over our lives in such an unhealthy way?

For example, how could I have allowed Cara, a twenty-year-old from Provo, to wrestle my five-year-old son to the ground and give him noogies on the top of his head until his hair actually thinned? And how could I have suffered her playing my John Lennon albums backwards, night after night, listening for a Satanic message? Why didn't I just give her a few beaver pelts and send her back to the salt flats? Was I afraid that Cara would quit and I would have to go through the entire process of finding another nanny? I'm ashamed to admit it, but it's the latter.

The irony of this whole situation is that I purposely waited until I was thirty-five to have a baby so that I would have the patience and the maturity to nourish my son so that he could grow up with a positive and loving attitude toward the world he lived in. Simply, I wanted him to have everything I didn't. I grew up a serf to a brother who ran a fascist dictatorship from his bunk bed.

The situation was exacerbated during my years in parochial

school. The newly built parish was taught by Polish nuns who left their homeland in 1952 when relations with the Vatican were severed, and the Catholic Church became a chief target of government persecution.

With a basic knowledge of the English language, they ran the school like Teutonic knights gaining a foothold in the pagan territory of Cleveland Heights. My first two years in school I didn't understand them and they didn't understand me. But by third grade, I lost my Midwest twang and spoke like Meryl Streep in *Sophie's Choice*. Fortunately I had a flair for accents. Listening to my Irish and Italian relatives sparring at the dinner table every Sunday gave me a sharp ear. I, however, had *no* flair for math. I used to walk home with echos of Sister Mary Agnes shouting in a thick tongue: "Dupa, if the Baby Jesus had twelve kielbasas and Judas stole ten, how many kielbasas did the Baby Jesus have left?"

"I do not know from that question, Sister," I replied in my strange Polish accent.

"Maybe you know from *this*, Dupa!" she said yanking at my braids.

It was because of my background that I was so intent on finding the perfect nanny to nurture my son's growing mind. But with every nanny who didn't work out, I began to slowly adjust my standards. By the time Nanny Number Eight moved out of the guest room with my fake Rolex, English as a first language was no longer a priority.

Mrs. Hollenbeck sent us a twenty-two-year-old French girl from Versailles, Claudine, a descendent of Louis XIV, the "Sun King," who built the manse.

"Her father is a master-chef at the *famous* La Table du Roi," Mrs. Hollenbeck said as if that was supposed to clinch the deal.

"Claudine," I said the day her boyfriend Jacques brought her for an interview, "do you like children?"

Jacques translated.

"Oui," she snapped.

"Terrific," I said, wondering if she'd bought the Madonna halter here or in Paris.

"And you can drive?" I asked.

Jacques translated.

"Pfffff," she said.

"But of course she can drive," Jacques said, also making a "Pfffff," sound.

After a few more questions, I asked if Claudine had anything she'd like to ask me.

"Quel jour la femme de menage fait elle la lessive?"

Jacques stroked her fashionably torn Levi's and translated, "Which day does your cleaning lady do laundry?"

Was I on "Candid Camera"?

"Claudine," Jacques said, his thick fingers an inch from the studs on her left breast, "never works on Saturday or Sunday."

"*Oui*," I said as Marie Antoinette rattled off French fast and furious: *"Mercredi après-midi je vais chez l'estheticienne."*

Jacques interpreted: "On Wednesday I go to the esthetician."

Could she be pushing this?

"Jacques," I said, "does she cook?"

Claudine puffed out her already pouty lips and said: *"Je n'ai jamais eu besoin de faire la cuisine, car mon pere est chef de cuisine."*

"What did she say, Jacques?"

"I never needed to cook in my life. My father is a master-chef."

"Claudine," I said, "how soon can you start?"

Now, three years later, I woke up to the sound of reveille, followed by Margaret shouting orders.

"Cruit, you got three minutes to get your butt out of that bunk, and five minutes to chow down! You read me?

"Fuckin' A," Chris said, dragging himself out of bed.

"Hey it's Saturday Sarge, why do I have to get up?"

"Quiet in the ranks!" Margaret barked. "We have a mall manuever."

"What about our counterinsurgency biltzkrieg at the playground?"

"The X.O. needs bunk sheets at Macy's White Sale."

"I hate shopping!" Chris whined.

"Cruit, I get my orders—you get yours!"

While Chris and Margaret were having breakfast, I heard Chris confide, "Sarge, I'm in real trouble."

"Spill your guts!" said Sargeant June Cleaver.

"I got kicked off the school bus for two weeks."

"Cruit, you shittin' me?"

"Sarge, it wasn't my fault," Chris whined. "You know that pussywimp Brandon? Every day I get on the bus he asks me math questions, and if I don't know the answer he starts laughing and gets the whole bus to laugh at me. Yesterday when I got on he asked me how much nine times nine was. I didn't know, and when he started laughing I got up and punched him out. He kicked me in the *balls!* Then we started rolling up and down the aisle wrestling it out. The bus driver turned us in to the principal. And now I'm kicked off the bus for two weeks." Chris's voice trailed off. "If the C.O. finds out, my ass is grass! He's a Quaker!"

"We'll plan the best method of action while we're at the mall. Then we'll chow down at McDonald's, arrive back on base at 1300, and bite the bullet."

"Sarge, I wish *you* had been on the bus. *You* would have taken care of that little pig! Wouldn't you?"

"Get in the Mustang, Cruit. And remember—never wrestle with a pig. You both get dirty and the pig likes it."

CHAPTER 5

THERE WAS NEVER any mention of the bus saga from either Margaret or Chris. Every morning for the following two weeks, Margaret gave Chris a lift to and from school. She gave no reason. I asked no questions.

Two weeks before Memorial Day, I received a letter from my mother thanking me for sending the photos of Chris and Margaret on the playground. That's how the letter began. It ended with her hauling me over the coals for hiring an "Army drill sergeant" to take care of her grandson.

She wrote:

"Liz, I'm well aware that you feel a need to pursue a career, but God forbid, to leave your only child—my only grandson— with a nanny who wears Army boots and carries a canteen around her waist! What kind of message is that for Chris? . . ."

I didn't take too much stock of what she said. Before I had nannies to occupy her every waking thought, she had John. Her comments were usually along the lines of: "Liz, when is that man going to get a job?" or "Does he sleep all day?" or "Liz, who is that other eccentric writer who shot himself in the head, leaving behind a young wife?" Although John had written over twenty books, he didn't become a worthwhile person until she saw him being interviewed about one of his books on Johnny Carson sandwiched between Charo and a chimp act.

Suddenly my husband had titanic clout. She no longer referred to John as "My daughter's *first* husband."

My mother's letter went on to say that she and my father would be driving up for the long Memorial Day weekend. She wrapped it up by reminding me of Eco-Ellie.

Ecosystem Ellie was Nanny Number Nine.

Eco-Ellie had a theory that she unfortunately shared with my mother. According to Ellie, if you don't clean a house for seven years, it automatically becomes self-cleaning. There's a balanced ecosystem. The microorganisms decompose new materials as quickly as they're added. Prey and predators (cats and mice) are in equal balance. Everything grows, dies, flourishes, decomposes. Complete life cycles of plants and animals go on uninterrupted in the corners of rooms, under the beds, and behind the refrigerator. "The trick," Ellie told my mother at the dinner table, "is to not lose your nerve, and give up after five or six years."

Ellie did not know her audience. My mother believed that God gave us two hands—one for Windex, and one for Pledge, and ten fingers to work to the bone.

My father left my house convinced that he had picked up something.

It's a good thing they weren't around the day John caught Ellie giving Chris moldy cheese and crackers to get rid of his cold.

"Ellie," Chris said, coughing, "what's all this disgusting green fuzzy stuff on my cheese?"

"Mold," Ellie said, moving about the kitchen in her Birkenstock sandals, "it's penicillin. It's good for you."

That got John's attention. "Christ!" John shouted above the U2 CD, "there's enough mold on that cheese to cure every lab rat in Connecticut!"

He turned to me and said, "The next thing, she's going to be taking him out into the woods for milk and mushrooms."

John tossed the cheese into the trash.

Ellie glowered at him from behind her John Lennons. Then

she reached into the trash and plucked out the moldy cheese. "For my compost heap," she said only to me.

"Ellie," I said, "Why don't you and Chris go play ball, I'll make lunch."

"Compost heap!" John gasped. "That'll attract every rabid raccoon in the neighborhood."

"Ellie put in a small organic garden," I explained. John was washing down the kitchen counter with Clorox.

"So that's what's been causing that stench wafting into my office."

"It doesn't smell."

"Liz, why are you defending her? She's turned our house into a fungus factory!"

"I'm not defending her. I'm being diplomatic."

"What's that supposed to mean?"

"She's just one of those well-meaning crunchy granola types who's heavy into ecology."

"Well I don't like her holier-than-thou attitude," John said. "I've written more books dealing with the environment than she's read!"

"You're overreacting!" I said. "She's simply a twenty-year-old girl with a cause."

"With a cause to squander our money at that beansprout store in town!"

I knew it was only a matter of time before John brought up the newly opened charge account at The Organic Gourmet. I wasn't sure if he was more burned over the monthly bill or the health food.

The only time I got John into a health-food store, the clerk reached into a barrel, saw a mouse scrambling about in the bulgur wheat, and jumped back, crunching John's foot with her earth shoes.

"Liz, do you know what last month's charge was?"

"I'll speak to her," I said. "Now give it a rest!"

I didn't tell John that every time she grabbed the car keys and her Guatemalan knapsack, I warned her to go easy on the pricey imported figs and seaweed. She promised that she would as soon as her garden began to produce. From the total on the bill, I guessed her garden and the indoor lemon and fig trees had a way to go.

"And I want to know where my chicken pot pies are?" John said.

"Aren't they in the freezer?" I asked, stalling for time.

"They're in her compost heap, aren't they?"

"They are definitely *not* in her compost heap. Darling, do you know what kind of artificial ingredients are in those things? Those chickens are lethal! They don't have the advantage of running around outside a cage eating real food. They're not hand-killed or hand-cleaned. They're pumped full of antibiotics and steroids and . . ."

"Liz, you're a sick woman!"

For the rest of the day John refused to talk to me. I knew that by bedtime we would be chatting as if those pot pies were still in the fridge. He was bullheaded about his culinary prefer-ences, which I must admit had a very wide range. John was proud of the fact that he could whip up a three-course meal in a pot of boiling water—a can of corned-beef hash, a can of peas, and a can of potatoes brought to a full boil for twenty minutes.

When I first visited John in the cottage where we now live, his refrigerator was bare except for a bottle of beer and one hot dog. That always stuck with me. I had never met a writer before John. I always imagined, however, that that's how one might live, no frills. Maybe that's what attracted me to John—his craggy earthiness. Then again, he could boil the dog food one night, and the next, take me to the finest French restaurant, and know just the perfect wine to order.

Whenever we'd have a spat, I would long for the days when John and I would travel half the year on research, just the two of us, a couple of Sony tape recorders tucked inside Abercrom-bie & Fitch shoulder bags, and a manual typewriter. One month we might be with climbers in the Swiss Alps, and the next investigating a chemical explosion in Northern Italy that wiped out a whole town, forever. Or another time, we'd be in a Himalayan monastery meditating with the monks, attempting to strike a balance between Western materialism and Eastern mysticism. We were deep. Our lives were rich. We weren't swallowed up in petty arguments over a nanny. We weren't bickering about how much time Chris was spending in front of Nintendo or doing a trip on ourselves because Chris nudged a kid off the balance beam in cold blood. Was his sudden aggressiveness just his age or was it genetic? Which relative was a sociopath?

Slowly and insidiously we had become bogged down in parenthood, insulating ourselves from a greater reality. After Christopher's birth, John stopped accepting overseas assignments. God forbid, anything could happen. The plane could crash. There could be a putsch, an earthquake, a satellite could drop out of the sky, and more. No longer was I preoccupied with trying to connect with the Oneness of the Universe. Emerson's essays were only distant memories. I no longer went to the Transcendentalist for comfort, but to trendy handbooks with chapters on: What to do if your child lies. What's a pushy parent? Counteraggression. The coup de grâce was when I stuck the Poison Control hot-line number over the reservation number for Chez Pierre.

I stopped reading the New York *Times,* and I began to believe that Mister Rogers really was talking to me when he sang: "Your body is perfect and so is mine." John and I began quoting Oscar the Grouch as if he were Sartre. The pathetic part about all of this was: we didn't even recognize what was happening to us. It took Birgit—the Swedish bombshell to shock us back into the world of grownups.

Birgit was one of Margaret's predecessors. There was no doubt about it, she was gorgeous, and she was after my husband.

Although John denied she had any interest in him, a woman always knows. It's primitive. So why did I hire Birgit in the first place? Was it because I was terrificially secure with my own looks? Wrong. It was simply because I didn't for one minute

No sooner had Birgit pinned up a gigantic poster of the Chippendale
Dancers and stored her athletic equipment than she was telling
my husband John that she would be "pleasured" to read
some of his books.

think that Birgit would even acknowledge John's presence, let alone his khaki-clad body.

No sooner did Birgit pin up a gigantic poster of the Chippendale dancers, store her weights, soccer ball, rollerblades, helmet, mountain bike, and Joe Weider Power Drinks, than she began asking John questions about the *incredible* process of writing a book.

"There is nothing I admire more than a writer of fine literature," she said in a choppy accent.

For a writer those words were as seductive as, "I haven't been laid since I left Stockholm."

"Well, you must be a student of literature?" John asked, slipping off his glasses as if that made him look thirty-five.

"I have read many books by your Mr. Hemingway," Birgit said. She tossed her natural blonde hair from one bouncy breast to the other and added, "I would be pleasured to read some of *your* books."

"I'd be flattered," John said.

Swell. She'd be "pleasured," he'd be "flattered," and I wanted to throw up.

The first month Birgit was with us she read about four paragraphs of one of John's books. It was more than enough to keep the communication between them alive.

"So, Birgit," John said with his glasses off, "read anymore of my book?"

"I adores the photograph of you on the jacket cover," Birgit responded. "You are what we call in Sweden 'snygg.'"

"That sounds like snot!" Christopher said, picking out the onions from Birgit's Swedish meatballs.

"'Snygg'?" I said, looking from Birgit to John. He was shamelessly basking in the adoration.

"Handsome," Birgit said.

I was dangerously close to the cutlery drawer.

"Let's see," John said, throwing out his lower jaw, "I think that photo was taken along the Amazon when I was researching a fascinating story about . . ."

Christ, he was pulling out all the stops to impress a girl who had crayon cramps.

"Darling," I said, "I took that photo of you down by our river. I distinctly remember the exact day. You had just come from the doctor, and you got the unfortunate news that you had a slipped disc . . . ."

"Dad, you promised you'd pitch some balls to me!" Chris interrupted. Poor child didn't even know that his father's life was in danger, and his mother was about to share a cell with Jean Harris.

"Okay, champ!" John said, "we'll give Birgit a well-deserved rest."

"Don't exert yourself!" I called. "You know what Dr. Steinberg said!"

For a split second I wanted to see the man I loved more than anything in the world keel over in front of Lolita. Instead he jogged out the front door, calling to us, "If you girls get bored, come on out and we'll have a game!"

How long could a reasonable human being let this go on? Until he pitched ten balls, that's how long. That would give me all the time I needed to tell Birgit to lay off my husband.

I went to Birgit's room, which looked like Herman's Sporting World, and spelled it out: "Birgit, why don't you get yourself a boyfriend who's not married!"

She looked up at me and burst into tears. My God, I thought, this is just like the movies. She's going to tell me that she and John are madly in love and will be living on a houseboat in Stockholm. Were there houseboats in Stockholm? John always wanted to live on a houseboat. I hated boats. That was it. I hated boats. He was dumping me. I didn't like the sun. It aged me. Birgit loved the sun. Jesus, this isn't really happening.

Birgit had thrown herself onto her bed and smothered her face in a pile of neon bike pants. She was out of control.

"Say it, Birgit!" I demanded. "Just *say* it!"

"I'm pregnant," she wept.

Oh, Jesus. Robin Williams married his nanny. There was

somebody else famous who just took off with his nanny. Get a grip, Liz.

"What are your plans, Birgit?" I asked, feigning control.

"I believed he loved me! I gave my body and my soul to him!" said this young melodramatic Ingrid Bergman.

"How long has this been going on?" I barked. "Did it start the weekend I took my mother into New York for her birthday?"

Birgit wiped her eyes with a hot pink jog bra, and then began to count out the weeks in Swedish, "Ett, tva, tre. Flag Day. Our national holiday. Six weeks ago. I want to kill him!"

I thought: Six weeks ago? Birgit was back in Stockholm six weeks ago.

"Birgit," I asked, feeling the weight of Sweden slip off my shoulders, "*who* do you want to kill?"

"Lars-Eric!" she exploded. "I want to kill him!"

That night Birgit showed me a letter she had written to that swine, Lars-Eric.

> Dear Lars-Eric:
> Today I go to the pharmacy and buy Clearblue Easy. Unique one-piece test—clear results in 3 minutes. Laboratory tests have shown it to be more than 99% accurate. How does it work? Clearblue Easy is able to detect tiny amounts of the hormone HCG in your urine. Can I get a false or misleading result? This should not happen if you follow the instructions correctly . . ."

"Birgit," I said, "This letter says absolutely *nothing* about you being pregnant. All you've done is copy the instructions off the home pregnancy test. There is not *one* mention of the word pregnant in the entire letter."

"Lars-Eric is a man of many tempers," she said.

Birgit confided that Lars-Eric had been a weightlifter and chosen for the Swedish Olympic squad after having defeated a well-known Bulgarian. Lars-Eric, however, was dropped from his team after testing positive for steroids. "After that time,"

Birgit explained, "Lars-Eric became a most suspicious and jealous man."

She went on to say, "One evening, Luther, a jazz musician, was playing at the hotel where I worked. He drove me home in a storm of snow. But first we stopped by Sweden's most beautiful Lake Mälaren to admire the huge snow flakes. Luther had a sunroof on his Saab. The snowflakes danced all over our faces," Birgit said in between jerky tears. "When we finally got to my family home, Lars-Eric was hiding behind a bush. He became insane with jealousy and put Luther's fine hands under the snow and then jumped on them. He cracked all his fingers as if they were mere chicken bones."

"Birgit," I said, "do you love this brute?"

Birgit nodded. "Liz, can you *please* help me write a letter?"

"Of course," I said, "but we're not going to mince words. It's his baby too."

"I hope so," Birgit said.

"You hope what?"

Birgit tugged at her Nike compression shorts and blurted: "It could be Luther's baby."

"Luther?"

"Luther, the musician," Birgit said, stroking a stuffed soccer ball pillow. "He plays the upright bass at the Blue Note in Stockholm. He is so brilliant. And he is so black."

"Birgit, you are in deep shit!"

Later that evening we sat down at the computer and composed an all-purpose letter and sent it to both Lars-Eric and Luther. The only thing changed were the names. The wording was a bit tricky.

Dear ——————:

I have some important news for you. I am 6 weeks pregnant. At this point in time, I don't know if I will keep the baby. A lot depends on your reaction. I love children. It does not matter if they are white, black, red or yellow. I love them all.

NANNIES

Darling, I miss you so much. I know we could be great parents to our child. He/She will be strong but sensitive to the arts.

I will anxiously await your reply. All my love,

Birgit

Before we sent the letters, I asked Birgit if there was anyone else she might like to send a copy to. She thought for a moment, and said tentatively: "No."

Relieved, I took them to the post office.

The upshot of the letters: Lars-Eric wrote and said that the baby couldn't be his. He was sterile from all the steroids he'd been taking.

Luther wrote and said that he'd been out of work for six months because of crushed fingers on both hands. "I still have to pick up a cup of coffee and drink it with my wrists," he wrote, adding, "My bass is gathering dust, and a family of spiders is living in the F-holes. The doctor asked how good a singer I was." He ended his rather curt letter by reminding Birgit that he had had a vasectomy ten years earlier.

Shortly thereafter, Birgit swilled an entire bottle of aquavit, and went on a graffiti rampage, writing "fuck" in Swedish all over her bedroom and bathroom walls. John assessed the damage, and then gave her a super-saver flight back to Stockholm.

After Birgit left we had her room painted and the carpet cleaned. Joe Weider Power Drinks can really do a number on cut pile.

CHAPTER 6

So HOW DID Birgit shock us back into the world of grownups? Birgit was the catalyst for me to take a long, hard look at myself. I wasn't that thrilled with what I saw. I had become petty and preoccupied with things of no consequence. Can you really throw washable silk into the machine? Was I truly an autumn? Did my upper arms have the old-lady-sag yet?

I was bored with myself and I was bored with John. But when Birgit arrived on the scene, and began the "snygg" schtick, and John rolled around in it like a dog in heat, I knew something had to change. I would have to make myself more exciting.

Part of me wanted to dump John and go live in Australia's Outback. I'd look for Crocodile Dundee. I'd find someone with whom I could wrestle crocodiles, drive a Jeep through mud, tame rattlesnakes. I'd live in torn jeans. Let my hair go gray. Well, maybe not that. I'd pitch my three jars of Estée Lauder skin-perfecting creme. I wanted to feel good about the real me. It was time for adventure! And one evening, I told John this.

"Liz," he said, "you've been smoking something."

In spite of John's cynicism, I knew he wanted adventure, too. After thirteen years of marriage, I knew him better than he knew himself. He was as bored as I. Only he wouldn't admit it.

Several weeks after Birgit was back in Stockholm, John hollered down from his office: "Lizzy, pack your knapsack!"

"Pack my what?" I called back. I was reading a letter from Birgit. She was living with Nels Nordstrom—the pastry chef at the hotel where she once worked. It was Nels's baby, and they were getting married. Could I please send her Chippendale poster?

"Pack your knapsack!" John said. "We're going to New Guinea to check out the headhunters! I just accepted an assignment."

New Guinea? Headhunters? Where was New Guinea? What about headhunters? Before Christopher was born, I would have known where New Guinea was, and what headhunters were. But now, my mind flashed to headhunters as recruiters who *place* executives, not savages who *eat* them.

Less than a month later, John and I boarded Garuda Airlines in Los Angeles for West Irian, New Guinea. Loaded down with those dusted-off Abercrombie & Fitch shoulder bags, stuffed with Sony TC–55s, malaria tablets, insect repellent and bee-keeper helmets, we manuevered our way down the narrow aisle to Seats 38 A and B, the tail of the plane. There's always something left of the tail.

Once again I was alive. I wasn't on my way to the principal's office to discuss Chris's chronic use of "Knullar fröken." I was on my way to research and write about a Stone-Age civilization where headhunting was no idle rumor.

As the 747 lumbered down the runway, I recalled Thoreau: "I want to live fully, and not when I come to die discover that I have not lived. Living is so dear. I want to suck out all the marrow of life and drive it into a corner."

By the time the "fasten the seat belt" sign was turned off, my mind had switched from "sucking the marrow out of life" to Jessica and my mother.

Jessica was a twenty-four-year-old nanny from Utah. She had worked for a friend of a friend. She came highly, *highly* recommended. She didn't hang on the phone all day and go out all night. She liked to spend her off hours alone in her room reading and writing. She had been an honor student at a Bible college. She drove stick shift. She was tidy.

Because of past experiences, I wasn't taking any chances. I arranged for my mother and father to drive up and be more or less floor managers for our month-long journey halfway around the world.

I guess I was more concerned about my mother than about Jessica. My mother has resented every nanny we've ever had. For some reason she felt as if her position as grandmother was threatened. Although the day she learned that I was pregnant, she said: "I'm telling you right now—hire good help. Don't entertain any ideas about dumping the baby with your father and me when you and John go off God knows where. We've put in our time . . ."

My mother does not remember ever saying that. Her selective memory is staggering. She can remember the name of every creep I ever went out with beginning in seventh grade. She has some sort of eerie random access memory that allows her to recall in which month and which year I was dumped by which greaser. She can call up in precise detail that Christmas, 1964, I bought Nick Cusio a thirty-dollar I.D. bracelet, engraved with the Elvis lyric: "Love Me Tonight." Cusio arrived at my house on Christmas Eve, wearing a black leather jacket, rat killers from Thom McAn, and Vitalis hair tonic that made my grandmother ill. He gave me a dollar bottle of Evening in Paris toilet water that was sold in Walgreen's next to the Odor-Eaters.

What is so unusual about her startling recall is that every year she sends me a birthday card on my brother's birthday.

I was jolted out of this reverie when the captain announced, an hour out of L.A.: "Ladies and gentlemen, we have a low-oil-pressure indicating-light on the Number Two engine. We're returning to Los Angeles so maintenance can take a look at it. This is not of undue concern. However, with safety in mind, we think it best to have it looked at."

Please do, I thought to myself. As a former flight attendant, I was all too familiar with the reassuring euphemisms. During my seven-year stint for Northwest, half of our captains sounded like Gomer Pyle during emergencies. "Gollll-ly, if ya look off to yer right, you'll see a real nice flame comin' out of the Number Two engine. So we're just gonna turn this baby back to the Twin Cities and have her looked at."

I'm not saying this approach is wrong. In fact, from my experience, it's comforting for passengers to think that the captain is so cool. I had some close brushes with death but that was almost ten years ago. Now I was a passenger on Garuda Airlines on my way back to Los Angeles with three hundred other edgy passengers and a husband squeezing my fingers.

"Jesus, I hate flying," said my Crocodile Dundee.

While the engine was being checked, I phoned home.

Christopher answered: "Mom," he said, breathless, "Grandma won't let Jessica take me to McDonald's!"

"Sweetheart," I said, "put Grandma on."

"Mom?" I asked, "is something wrong?"

"No, honey," she said. "Are you in Guyana yet?"

"It's New Guinea, Mom." I didn't bother to remind her that we had a fourteen-hour plane ride ahead of us. And I certainly didn't tell her about the engine.

My father got on the extension, "Is your flight delayed?" he asked. "According to my calculations, you're supposed to be halfway to Hawaii." I was glad he wasn't doing the navigating.

Chris got on another extension.

"Mom, tell Grandma it's okay for Jessica to take me to Mc-Donalds!"

My mother lowered her voice. "Your father's nervous about her driving."

My father lowered his voice: "She pulls out of the driveway like a bat out of hell."

Chris barked: "Knullar fröken!"

"Enough of that!" I snapped. "Do you understand me, young man?"

"Ja," he said, a perfect imitation of Birgit.

"What language is he speaking now?" my mother asked.

"Swedish," I told my mother.

"Gee," she said, "I remember when you were his age, you used to speak with that ridiculous Polish accent."

"We'll all go to McDonald's, and I'll drive," my father said.

"Perfect," I said, motioning to John at the gate that everything at home was okay.

"I can't eat that greasy food," my mother complained.

"Have one of their salads," my father said.

"I'm not eating that brown, wilted lettuce."

"Grandma," Chris said, now being the mature one, "we'll go to Burger King."

"The last time we came up your grandfather chipped his tooth at that place."

"That was at Wendy's," my father said.

"We'll go to McDonald's," my mother said, as if she had just thought of it.

"I'm going to fix your garbage bin," my father said.

"Not before McDonald's," my mother said, adding, "Liz, what's the name of that place you're going to?"

"New Guinea, Mom. They just announced the flight's boarding. I'd better run."

"Have fun, honey. You're not to worry about a thing. And buy yourself something cute with that money I gave you."

"Like a cute shrunken head?" I asked.

"You decide," she said, oblivious to life outside Cleveland Heights.

"Where do you keep your tools?" my father wanted to know.

"On the floor beside the bookshelves. Dad, I gotta go."

My father chuckled, "Most people keep tools in the garage."

I hung up, trying to once again get into the "sucking the marrow out of life" spirit.

CHAPTER 7

"Duck!" John yelled. He yanked me down to the floor of the rubber Zodiac. In moments there were spears flying in every direction.

"What's happening?" I called above wild war cries that were too close for comfort.

"Stay low!" our guide commanded. Then he shouted something in a strange language. For a moment there was a deadly silence.

A rhythmic chanting began.

"You can get up now," the guide said.

There were six elaborately carved canoes surrounding our small rubber boat. Each canoe carried about a dozen warriors in full war paint. Their noses were punctured with huge bone ornaments, smack out of *National Geographic*. From the neck down they were naked, except for penis sheaths that looked like horns tilted heavenward.

"Should I smile and wave?" I whispered to John who was fumbling with the Sony TC-55, moments before it was scooped out of his hand by a curious warrior who had leaped onto our Zodiac with the balance of a tightrope walker.

"Show him how it works," the guide said.

John's trembling hands made it difficult for him to press the on-off button. Mine were no better.

We had reason to tremble. The evening before we set out, our guide told us that our visit might be risky.

"What do you mean, risky?" John asked, sipping an extra-dry Beefeater martini. We were aboard the Lindblad *Explorer*, anchored in the Spice Islands, waiting for the torrential rains to let up so that we could make the four-hour Zodiac trip into Asmat territory.

"As you probably already know," the New Zealand guide began, "where we're going is the site where Michael Rockefeller disappeared."

"A victim of the headhunters?" I asked, tasting the Australian Chardonnay.

"Well," the guide said, shaking his head from side to side. He was on a search for the priceless art and wood carvings of the Asmats. At first he was thought to have drowned when his canoe overturned. Later, it was rumored that he had done them a wrong turn. So they paid him back Asmat-style."

"But that was back in the early sixties," I said, as if they had given up headhunting for mah-jongg.

"Three days ago," the guide said with *no* inflection in his voice, "three Catholic missionaries were beheaded."

I looked over at John. He was scribbling notes.

"We have a young son," I whined.

"So do I," the guide said, proudly. "Does he play soccer?"

I nodded, and it was back to business.

"If proper protocol is followed," the guide said, "there is nothing to fear. Except in the case of an intervillage war, which I must warn you is not an infrequent occurrence. We *must* take precautions as to which villages we visit."

"Why is that?" John said.

"Tribal rivalries and jealousies."

"What's proper protocol?" I asked, wondering what Christopher was doing. Was it his bedtime? Or was he at school? Was Jessica still pulling out of the driveway like a bat out of hell? Had my mother figured out what "Knullar fröken" meant? Had my father built a garage for the tools? I even thought about Holly and her pet bird, Mr. Unger.

"Protocol," the guide told us, "could entail, depending on the ceremony, sucking the breasts of the wives of the chief until milk comes and kissing the armpits of the chief himself."

John cleared his throat and said: "I've had camel's milk along the Khyber Pass, rattlesnake in the Amazon, and rat in the Sudan."

"And you had the nerve to complain about Eco-Ellie's eggplant parmigiana?"

"Liz, that was disgusting!"

Halfway up the river, another armada of war canoes appeared. They were manned by equally fierce-looking warriors. In minutes the two fleets were engaged in some sort of battle, throwing white lime powder and palm shoots at each other, and shouting.

"Nothing to worry about mates," our guide said, "it's a welcoming."

All I could think about were those Saturday mornings back in the fifties, sitting in front of the seven-inch Philco with my brother Gary, watching the Wild Man of Borneo on the "Andy Devine Show." Afterwards, Gary and I would go into the backyard, pretending we were in the Borneo jungle. Gary would carry a branch as if it were a spear, chant "cowabunga," and chase me around until my mother called out the kitchen window that if we didn't shut up we'd wake up old Viola Preuss next door.

Now, we were only miles from Borneo, and according to our guide: "Borneo is actually quite civilized compared to where we'll be going."

His last words to us as we beached the Zodiac were: "I want to caution you once again that this could be dangerous territory if proper protocol is not followed."

I stepped out from the Zodiac, and immediately sank ankle deep in mud, temporarily losing one Reebok. Two topless women, chewing betel nut, laughed uproariously while a young man in the biggest penis sheath I'd ever seen (I was now an expert) plucked me up onto more solid ground.

"Nice penis sheath," I was tempted to say.

"Thank you," I said, nodding and smiling, and trying to avoid looking south of the border.

"Bohumkumba," he said, adjusting his nose bone.

"Yes," I said, my eyes searching furtively for John and our guide. "I wonder where my husband went? We seem to have gotten separated."

"Ahumcabaca," he replied.

"I think I'll just mosey over to those mud huts and see if he's there."

"Juba-Juba."

"He's wearing khaki," I said to the Stone-Age man.

My T-shirt had gotten wet, and it was clinging. I crossed my arms, and headed up a small embankment to where some sort of ritual was taking place. Mostly women and children were dancing in a circle to the sound of drums and chanting.

The warrior was clamped at my side, his delicately carved penis sheath bouncing up and down as he kept time to the beat. It was catchy. I found myself walking with a little jaunt, too. I just wished I could have spotted John or our guide.

I was searching the distance when suddenly a group of women and children closed in on me. They were tugging at my long strawberry blonde hair. An elderly lady with breasts scraping the ground, pulled my head down and inspected my scalp. For a brief second, I wondered if she were checking to see if it was time for my roots to be done. Mr. Anthony always did that. Several were scratching at my skin, apparently trying to see what was underneath the white.

"Ouch!" I cried.

My warrior friend shooed them away with the tip of his spear. "Obo-Obo!"

"Thanks," I said. "That really hurt."

The next thing I knew, my new-found pal was leading me down a mud path lined with sago trees. Although we didn't understand one another, I had some silly notion that he was taking me to my husband.

There was a pungent odor everywhere. But it wasn't unpleasant. It smelled like a combination of burning leaves and charred meat. My heart was racing along with my imagination. Charred meat?

We were getting farther and farther away from the sounds of chanting and drums.

"My husband's gotta be around here somewhere" I said, as if he had a clue to what I was saying.

He picked up his pace as we neared a thatched mud hut that stood on stilts.

"Could John be in here?" I wondered.

He stroked his nose bone then motioned with his spear for me to go in first.

"Gee, thanks, but I think I'll just wait out here," I said. I thought my heart was going to pop through my wet T-shirt.

His eyes widened, his mouth tightened. Talk about universal expressions.

"Well, just for a minute," I said, cursing John and that guide for being wherever. I suddenly hoped that John had his head buried in some chief's armpit.

"Very charming," I said, standing in the doorway and scanning the hut. There was a straw mat on the dirt floor—not a stick of furniture anywhere to be seen. Maybe he just moved in?

"I'd love to stay, but . . ."

"Kognaga."

Either my eyes were playing tricks on me, or his penis sheath had more of a tilt to it.

"Kognaga," he repeated. Then he pointed with his spear for me to sit down on the mat.

"I've been sitting all morning," I said. "Four-hour Zodiac ride."

"Kognaga!"

"Oh, all right, But I *really* can't stay."

With that, he disappeared behind a straw curtain. I could make my escape. Where would I go? Where did he go? Was he freshening up? The humidity made my clothes stick. Why was I concerned about my clothes? He wanted my head.

I would have given my right arm—literally my right arm—to be back in Connecticut, driving Christopher to soccer and bitching about Birgit. I suddenly knew what Howard's wife, Janet, meant when she said: "I love the day-to-day drudgery of motherhood. Even when I go to Florida to visit my parents, I feel antsy for my own little nest. Howie hates it when I leave."

At the time she told me that, I thought: Yeah, when the snowbird's in the Boca condo, Howie's in the 750 thou passive-solar nest with one of his Nordic birds, hating every minute of it, counting the minutes until Janet and the two little savants return.

Now I had a handle on what she meant. At least the part about loving the day-to-day drudgery of motherhood. If I could have been content shuffling between soccer, baseball and Mc-Donald's, I wouldn't be in this predicament—forty nautical miles south of the equator in a mud hut with a fella probably changing into a more comfortable penis sheath.

How could I convey to this somewhat sexy Stone-Age man that my natural hair color was not strawberry blonde? How do you say "mouse brown" in Asmat? How could I let him know that L'Oréal haircolor fades dramatically in tropical sun? Shrunken, it's anybody's guess what the results might be. One year we went to St. Thomas and Mr. Anthony nearly shot me for not coating my hair with Paul Mitchell's supercharged conditioner while in the sun. "Our hair has been ruined!" he said, petulantly stomping his tan Ferragamo.

I reached into my Abercrombie bag and fished for a rubber band to tie my hair back. When I looked up I was shocked at the sight of the Asmat warrior emerging from behind the straw curtain. He was wearing a Yale T-shirt.

"Bahunga!" he said, pointing toward my shirt. It didn't take a Margaret Mead to determine that he didn't want my head, he wanted my Mickey Mouse T-shirt.

"I'd love to give it to you," I said, "but I don't have a change of clothes." I lowered my voice and added confidentially: "I'm not wearing a bra."

"Bahunga!" he repeated, whch I interpreted to mean: "Tough shit!"

I slipped off the shirt and passed it to him. The only thing he seemed interested in was the shirt. Then once again he disappeared behind the straw. Within seconds he was back. He was holding the most intricately carved statue. And he was wearing my T-shirt. Fortunately, it was a man's Large.

"That T-shirt goes great with your shell necklace," I said.

I suddenly recalled something else our guide had told us: The Asmat warriors keep track of how many heads they hunt by putting notches in their shell necklaces. My friend had four notches in his.

"Hungabunka," he said, passing the carving to me.

"Is this for me?" I asked. "But it's absolutely beautiful. You can't just give this to me."

After the transaction he seemed anxious for me to hit the road.

"Lizzy!" I heard off in the distance. "Lizzy! Where are you?"

"My husband's calling!" I said to my warrior friend.

He ignored me. He seemed totally involved with his new Mickey Mouse T-shirt. Other Asmats were coming up to him and fingering the 100% cotton. My bare chest was not given even as much as a glance.

"Elizabeth!" John shrieked when he saw me naked from the waist up, and standing next to probably the best looking Asmat in town. "Where's your shirt?"

"I traded it for this!" I said. "Isn't it just fantastic! It's a carving of a man on one end and a woman on the other holding a small child. It's you, me and Christopher. Don't you just love it?"

"For crying out loud, Liz, put this on." John said, ripping off his Khaki shirt while at the same time trying to cover my chest with his body—as if anybody cared.

Elizabeth Fuller

* * *

Weeks later, when we got to Bali, I phoned home. The instant my mother answered, I could tell that all was not well on the Western Front.

"Mom, something's wrong," I said.

There was a long, drawn out silence that spoke volumes.

"No, honey, everybody's just fine."

"Chris is behaving?" I asked.

"He's not the problem."

"It's Jessica?" I said.

"Don't you worry," my mother consoled. Then, on my dime, she proceeded to recap the saga.

"She's reading sex books all day long," she whispered.

"Mom," I said, "she's allowed to read whatever she likes."

"I want your father to get on the phone and tell you what else she's doing."

"I'm calling from Bali," I said to deaf ears.

"How's the weather over there?" my father screamed into the receiver.

"It's beautiful, Dad."

"Is your trip successful?" he asked.

"John and I have enough material for a dozen books. Dad what happened with Jessica?"

"That can wait," he said. In his next breath, he told me: "I was opening your bills—as you told me to—and I came across an eighty-dollar phone call to a 900 number. I called the operator, and she told me that the charges were to 1-900-Blow-n-Go."

"Oh, Jesus!" I said.

My father continued: "That night, your mother and I had a talk with Jessica. She denied having made the calls. But the very next night . . ."

"Dad," I said, a total wreck, "can this wait till we get back next week?"

"Sure," he said, "your mother and I have it under control."

My mother picked up the extension, "Did you tell Liz about the dirty phone calls to her boyfriends?"

64

John was tapping his watch. "Liz, it's costing us eight dollars a minute."

"Mom, Dad, I'll call you guys when we get back to Manila," I said, wishing I had never called in the first place. "Could you put Chris on for a second?"

"It's midnight" my father reprimanded in the exact same tone as when I was a teenager, sneaking into the house after curfew.

Before I hung up, my mother said: "While you're in Manila, you should look up that nanny who sent your good Krups cappuccino machine to her relatives."

"Good idea, Mom."

"*What* was a good idea?" John asked the moment I hung up.

"Oh, I don't know," I said. "You know the way my mother rambles."

I didn't want to remind John of Mary—the Philippine Philanthropist. Just before we left on our trip, John discovered his seasoned knapsack missing. He carried on more about that old, patched backpack than about the toaster oven that disappeared shortly after our Krups.

The investigative journalist was on my heels like a pit bull.

"Why did you say, 'Oh, Jesus?'" he asked, cutting into the complimentary mango.

"Well, if you must know, Jessica's not working out too well."

When I told John about the 1-900-Blow-n-Go charge, he nearly choked to death on mango seeds.

"Liz, this is serious!"

"Chill," I said. "My folks are handling it just fine."

"She's gotta go," John said. He grabbed the phone.

"It's past midnight!"

John dialed. On the first ring, Jessica picked up. The connection was scratchy. John could barely hear her. I'm sure his voice was muffled too.

"Hello, Jessica," John said.

"I'm butt naked," said the twenty-four-year-old honor student from the Bible college.

"Jessica, this is John Fuller!" he said, slow and loud.

She hung up.

I convinced John to let it ride until morning. He popped a Maalox tablet and we went to the beach to sort out our voluminous research notes.

The next day when we called home, my father said that early that morning Jessica had quit.

"It's impossible to witness about the Lord Jesus Christ to a family of swine," she said on her way out the door.

CHAPTER 8

Now, a year and some months later, I had more pressing matters on my mind than Jessica, headhunters and "sucking the marrow out of life." My mother was foremost in my thoughts. According to her letter and eight follow-up phone calls, she and my father were due to arrive in less than a week for the long Memorial Day weekend. If I knew my mother, she was probably sharpening her Lee Press-On Nails in preparation for meeting Margaret.

For most people, Memorial Day means beer on the boat, but for Margaret, it meant lining the driveway with a dozen flags and constructing a mini Fort Dix.

I was sitting at my desk staring at a blank screen on my Apple monitor when I heard what sounded like a jackhammer in the backyard. On closer inspection, Christopher and Margaret were chewing up the lower forty with a Rototiller of all things.

"What on earth's going on?" I called from my office window.

Margaret snapped to attention. "We're constructing an 'O' course to demonstrate Cruit's physical prowess to his grandparents next weekend, ma'am."

"A what?"

"An obstacle course, ma'am."

"Mom, wait till Grandma and Grandpa see what Sarge taught me?"

67

I was grateful that John was in Philadelphia. He was accepting a distinguished science award for his book on nuclear power.

"You're not going to dig up the yard too much?" I asked.

"Only enough to construct the course, ma'am."

Margaret and Chris were a real pair behind the Rototiller. They were both wearing camouflage cutoffs, work boots and U.S.S. *Arizona* baseball caps. Chris's cap was on backwards.

My first reaction had been to tell them to return the Rototiller to our next-door neighbor, and patch up the lawn, but their enthusiasm was contagious.

I found myself shutting down my computer to help make trenches, a climbing wall out of an old trestle partition, and balance beams out of two-by-fours. I watched in horror as the two suspended ropes from the oak tree on the riverbank. And I watched with pride as Margaret and Chris negotiated the sale of three barrels from a nursery in town. "How much those barrels going for, sir?" Margaret asked.

"Twelve bucks," the salty owner said. "You gonna pot geraniums?"

"We're going to crawl through them," Chris told the man.

Margaret, no stranger to a street market, said: "Those barrels aren't going to last till Labor Day. We'll give you twelve bucks for all three of them."

The owner shook his head, "No way."

Meanwhile Christopher was inspecting the barrels from all angles. "All those barrels have big cracks in the side, sir," Chris said, rolling his eyes toward Margaret.

"Six bucks apiece," the owner said.

"I've seen Swiss cheese with fewer holes," Margaret said. "Four bucks."

"Those barrels *new* cost me ten bucks apiece," the owner said, getting into the spirit.

"When they were new, they were probably worth it," Margaret said.

"Sarge, there's another flower store down the road," Chris said on cue.

"Five bucks," he said. "I'm givin' 'em away."

"Four," Margaret said. "They're firewood."

"Let's go," Chris said.

"All right," the owner said, half-amused, "three for twelve bucks."

"Thank you very much, sir," Chris and Margaret said simultaneously.

By the end of the week, Fort Dix had come to Connecticut.

When John returned from Philadelphia and saw the yard, he freaked. "They've dug into the septic system!"

"They did not!" I said, reminding John that the septic system was in the front yard.

The only thing that calmed John down was watching his son ace the obstacle course while Margaret timed him with a stopwatch.

"Five minutes and twelve seconds!" Margaret hollered to Chris as he dropped from the swinging rope into the river.

"Is that good?" said my drowned rat.

"For a fruitwhip!" Margaret called.

By the end of the day Chris's time was two minutes and seven seconds.

"Am I doin' good now, Sarge?"

"Fuckin' A!" Margaret said, not realizing that John and I were on the upper deck enjoying the show. "Cruit, you keep that up and you're headed for the Academy."

"Yes! Yes! Yes!" Chris said, doing some kind of power dance on the lawn.

I was in the kitchen basting a chicken with poor Mrs. Kibble's homemade barbeque sauce, when I heard my parents' station wagon pull into the driveway. Time to slip on the boxing gloves.

My mother got out of the car expecting Christopher to run to her with outstretched arms. Instead she was met with Christopher standing at parade rest between Margaret and the American flag.

"Cruit Christopher, reporting as ordered!" he said, snapping off a salute.

My mother looked like Harriet Nelson after Ricky said he was running away to join the circus.

"Give Grammy a big hug!" she said, slinging poison darts at Margaret.

"I can't break ranks, Grandma."

Margaret gave Chris the high sign. He broke loose and ran into her waiting arms.

"Look what Grammy brought you," she said, reaching into the back seat of the wagon. It was a stuffed panda.

"Grandma," Chris said, "this is for pussies."

Hearing that, my father cleared his throat, and lit a cigarette.

"Grandpa, I hope you're going to field-strip that butt!" Chris warned.

A smile broke across my father's face. "Yes, sir," he said swinging Chris into the air. "And after I field-strip this butt, I want to see you slam one out of the park."

"Tomorrow's the playoff," Chris said. "We're up against the best team in the league."

"I just saw a very scary piece on "60 Minutes" about how all these kids who play Little League are getting injured," my mother said."

"Mom, kids can get injured in their own backyard."

The moment those words left my lips, Chris said, "Hey, wait till you guys see me and Sarge's obstacle course."

Neither Chris nor Sarge had a clue as to what pleases a Cleveland Heights housewife.

"That child's going to kill himself!" my mother said as she watched Chris scale the wall, and then drop down and crawl through the barrels. "I can't watch this."

She went into the house to see if the Joe Weider stains came out of Birgit's rug. I never told her about the walls.

"So, did you ever find out what happened to Birgit?" my mother asked, examining the rug.

"According to her last letter, the baby was *definitely* Luther's. This did not sit too well with Nels."

"Let's see, Nels was the weightlifter?"

"Pastry chef," I said.

"And what's the latest on that dentist?" my mother asked, lighting a cigarette.

"Mom, when are you going to quit smoking?"

"Howard. The orthodontist. That's who I mean," she said, exhibiting her great capacity for selective listening. "What kind of no-good is he up to?"

"Wait till you hear this," I said, perking up her ears like a German shepherd. "Janet's paying him back."

"Divorce?"

"Jacuzzi repairman," I said.

"Noooo," my mother whispered. Her eyes were on fire. "How'd you find out?"

"I'll tell you the whole story. But first you have to promise to give Margaret a chance."

"Honey, you know I'm always fair."

"Mom, promise me."

"She's so Army."

"So what?" I said. "She's the best thing that's ever happened to Christopher. Even his teachers are impressed with his sudden maturity."

"Let's have cappuccino," she said, cutting me off. "I'm *dying* to hear all about Janet."

I frothed the milk, sprinkled chocolate and cinnamon on top and spilled out the news. "Chris and I were down at Coley Park. It was a half day of school. Chris was digging worms for his new fishing rod. I told him to look along the riverbank for night crawlers. It's very secluded."

"Don't ever let him go down there alone," my mother warned. "Places like that are crawling with perverts."

"He took off ahead of me. When I finally caught up, I came face to face with two people sprawled on a blanket. As Jessica might say, 'they were butt naked.' Next to them was a pile of clothes."

"Ohhhhhhh," my mother said.

"I turned and headed to the road."

"What about Chris? You didn't leave him down there alone?"

"I'm getting to that," I said. "I began calling him from the parking area. He couldn't hear with the sound of the river. So

71

I waited about five minutes—giving Romeo and Juliet time to get their clothes on—and went back. By that time they were dressed and sitting on the blanket drinking Pouilly Fuissé out of pink deco goblets. The empty wine bottle had lilacs in it. It was so romantic. Howard's been such a beast to her."

"Tit for tat," my mother said.

I went on: "The next day Janet called and wanted to meet at Oscar's for coffee."

"And?"

"She pretty much told me that she was in love with the guy. She said she feels like a teenager. Alive. She kept saying that it was so healthy. And when I asked what she meant, she confided real personal things about her and Howard."

"Oh?"

"I guess he has a rather strange sexual appetite."

"Oh?"

"Janet said that the only way he can—you know—have an orgasm, is for Janet to put on a long blonde wig, a little folk dress with matching babushka, wooden clogs and speak German."

"What a weirdo," my mother said, fanning herself.

"Janet had me hysterical. She said that during sex she says things in German like: 'I'm married to a flaming asshole.' And Howard goes crazy: 'Yes, baby,' he writhes, 'More. More. More.'"

"Imagine that," my mother said, slightly embarrassed.

"You know, Mom, before Janet told me all of this I really wasn't that crazy about her. But she's really got a great sense of humor."

"What about those flash cards?"

"She's given them up," I said. "She's devoting all of her free time to Danny."

"Danny?"

"You know, the Jacuzzi repairman."

"I just read where Liz Taylor's new boyfriend's a construction worker," my mother said. "She's skinny again. Mike Todd was the love of her life. Not Richard Burton. Mike Todd had all that strength that she needed."

I wasn't quite sure where she was going with all of this.

"Well, good for Janet," she said, back on target. "Does Howard suspect?"

"No," I said. "Howard's wrapped up in getting lingual appliance certification. And with trying to score with their latest nanny, Helga."

"What happened to Darlene?" my mother asked.

"She's back in California, trying to get on 'Jeopardy!'"

"Oh," my mother said, "So, tell me about Helga."

"She's a twenty-year-old from a Swiss farm who literally yodels herself to sleep."

"Just like Uncle Rocco and Aunt Rosie," my mother whispered.

"Uncle Rocco and Aunt Rosie yodel themselves to sleep?"

"Nooooo." She got up from the kitchen table and peered out the window to make sure my father was still in the backyard with Chris and Margaret. "I'm talking about extramarital affairs."

"Aunt Rosie," I said, "she's in a nursing home."

"That's now. But back when your father and I were first married, and she was still married to Nunzio . . ."

"The clothes designer who died on the ship returning from Italy?"

"That's not what really happened," my mother confessed. "Make us some more cappuccino and I'll tell you the whole story."

"Let's see," she began, "your father and I were married in 1944. Aunt Rosie and Nunzio were living on First Street. Oh, the house they had! It was gorgeous. Nunzio made good money. Italian marble everywhere! They had six kids. But he was a gambler. Was he ever handsome! He designed men's clothes at a factory in Cleveland—Merkle and Sons."

"I can't believe that we had a *designer* in our family," I said.

"A designer and a *cad*. Nunzio had an eye for the young girls. He even used to flirt with me when your father and I were first dating," she said with a girlish giggle.

"What a bounder!" I said. "You mentioned something about Nunzio *not* having died on the boat?"

"That's right," my mother said. She once again got up to make sure that my father was still outside. "Your father's family is so funny about keeping this deep, dark secret."

"I won't tell a soul. Scout's honor."

"Well, they lived in this big house and every so often they'd send for one of the relatives. They all came from Pozzuoli—a small, very poor town south of Naples. Sophia Loren came from there . . ."

"Holy cow, you think Nunzio was related to Sophia Loren?"

"Probably," my mother said for my benefit. "She's doing an eyeglass commercial now. She must have had two face-lifts. Now, where was I?"

"You said that they'd send for relatives."

"Oh, yes, one of those relatives who came to live with Aunt Rosie and Nunzio was Rocco."

"Uncle Rocco?"

"He wasn't your uncle then. He was living in the attic and working all day for Nunzio. Sewing. Every time your father and I would go there, he'd be sitting at a Singer Sewing machine, singing 'Arrivederci, Roma . . .'"

"Come on, Mom."

"I'm telling you the truth. That's what I remember most. He used to tease me because I was Irish. He'd say 'I a going to teacha you how to sing "Arrivederci, Roma."' Uncle Rocco wasn't as handsome as Nunzio, but he was a good, honest man. He loved the kids. Nunzio could have cared less. But Rocco, he always had a dozen kids tugging at him to play. Oh, he loved to have a good time. Could he dance! I remember the way Uncle Rocco and Aunt Rosie would fox-trot around the living room. They had a Victrola with a hand crank. They'd dance to Claudio Villa."

"Where was Nunzio when they were doing the ballroom dancing?"

"He was never home," she said. "Until Aunt Rosie hired Annamaria. A beautiful Italian girl from Naples."

"Annamaria?"

"A girl to look after the kids."

"A nanny?"

"They didn't call them nannies back then. But that's what she was."

"Why did she need someone to take care of the kids?"

"I'm about to tell you. Aunt Rosie's sister was dying. She had TB."

"In Pozzuoli?"

"In Trieste. Northern Italy. Aunt Rosie wanted to go back and be with her sister. After all, it was her sister. Nunzio wouldn't let her go alone."

"So Uncle Rocco went along?"

"Exactly. They sailed over on the *Augusto*. They were gone for *months*."

"And Nunzio was home with the beautiful nanny?"

"That's what happened," my mother said. "And when Aunt Rosie returned, Annamaria was wearing her clothes, her jewelry. She was even sleeping in their bed."

"Just like Howard and Elsa."

"Liz, there's nothing new under the sun."

"Did Aunt Rosie toss her out?" I asked.

"Back then you didn't do that. Catholics didn't get divorced. They all more or less tolerated each other. We all knew what was going on. But nobody said anything. And when Nunzio was only forty-six he was shot."

"What!"

"By his girlfriend's husband. A shoemaker at the May Company."

"Give me a break!"

"That's what happened," my mother said, polishing off the cappuccino. "They were in bed. Bang!"

"Dead?"

"May his soul rest in peace," my mother said. "It was in the Cleveland *Plain Dealer*."

"Was it Annamaria's husband?"

"Noooo. Annamaria only lasted a couple of years. He liked them young. But Aunt Rosie—with her heart like gold—let Annamaria live with them. How she looked after that girl."

75

"I don't ever remember an Annamaria," I said.

"Oh, you wouldn't. A few months after Nunzio died, Annamaria married one of his tailors. Aunt Rosie arranged it."

"Aunt Rosie was an Italian yenta," I said.

"A what?"

"Never mind, Mom. Go on with your story."

"Annamaria ended up moving to Sandusky. You weren't even born yet."

"And when did Aunt Rosie and Uncle Rocco get married?"

"Shortly after Nunzio died. They were married in Italy. Trieste. Your brother was just an infant."

"Sounds as if Aunt Rosie had an interesting life?"

"God bless her," my mother said making the sign of the cross. "Now the poor thing doesn't know who she is, where she is."

"Mom, I don't want that to happen to me. Don't all of our relatives go a little soft upstairs?"

"Pretty much," she said, resigned to the lousy gene pool.

For the first time since we returned from Indonesia, I thought about "sucking the marrow out of life."

"Liz," my mother said, rinsing the cups, "I know you were worried sick about John and Birgit."

"What?"

"I'm your mother. I know you."

"Mom, you're so off base," I said.

God, how did this Kreskin the Amazing who lives five hundred miles away know that I wanted to braid the Bombshell into a loaf of Swedish Julbrod?

"These young girls come here off farms to snatch a rich husband."

"We're not rich!"

"Compared to them you are," my mother said. "It doesn't matter if the man isn't young and good-looking."

Claw time.

"John is very attractive," I said. "But Birgit had *no* interest in my husband. And John certainly never gave her a second look!

Just the thought of it makes me want to burst out laughing. *Me* jealous of Birgit. Ha. Ha. Ha."

"I certainly don't think Margaret was a suitable replacement," my mother said, as she left the room to iron slacks for the next day's little league game.

Knullar fröken, I said to myself.

CHAPTER 9

"KNULLAR FRÖKEN," Chris mumbled as he struck out with two men on base.

"Nice try, Cruit!" Margaret said from behind the batter's cage. "Good eye."

"You'll get one next time, Cruit," John said, roughing up his hair. In the last few weeks, John had begun calling him Cruit, a fact that annoyed my mother no end.

"It's the bottom of the eighth, Sarge," Chris said, throwing off his helmet. "I blew it. They're winning 5 to 1."

Just then one of Chris's teammates, Kevin, popped one up. The inning ended. The opposing team and their parents were cheering loud and long. Kevin began to cry.

"Kevin," Margaret said, "you got a hit off a curve ball!"

"I did?" Kevin said, wiping tears with the sleeve of his Number 22 orange jersey.

"Fuckin' A," Christopher said, slapping Kevin a high five.

While the parents passed croissants and coffee, Margaret stood at parade rest. Occasionally she'd sip Gatorade from her canteen.

"Come on over and sit with us, Margaret!" I said from the bleachers. I was sandwiched between my folks. John was pacing between third and home. My mother was more concerned with Margaret's outfit than in watching the game.

NANNIES

"Why does she have to wear those ridiculous clothes? And those boots."

"Mom, they're fatigues. She likes to dress like that."

"Can't you give her some of your old clothes? You've got so many cute sundresses and sandals that you never wear."

"That would insult her," I said. "Now watch the game. Chris is on second base."

"I wish they'd play with a wiffle ball," my mother said.

"For chrissake, keep your eye on that ball!" hollered the man behind me in Bollé shades.

The kid turned to look at his father and missed the ball.

"Wake up, Derek!" the coach called.

"Strike two!"

"That was no strike!" the father said to his wife who was recording the event on the Sony Super 8.

"We can play it back," she said.

"Good idea," he said, looking through the viewfinder. "That was a ball."

"Tell the coach," the mother said.

"Let's wait and see how he calls the next one."

"Strike three!"

The green jersey dropped his bat and broke down in tears. The father marched onto the field. The Sony was slung over his shoulder. The coach looked through the viewfinder. A few words were exchanged. The kid on deck got up to bat. The father walked back shaking his head.

"Son of a bitch can't see," the father smoldered.

"Should we have him coached privately this summer?" the wife asked. "We've got six days between the Vineyard and soccer camp."

The green team went down in order.

"Mom, Chris is third to bat," I said. I got up and went over to the bench. "Hey, sport," I whispered, "do your best."

When it was Chris's turn to get on deck, one of the kids from the green team called over: "No batter!"

Before Chris had a chance to return the compliment, Marga-

79

When the air cleared, the rival coaches agreed that it had taken Margaret, an outsider, to remind them what the game of Little League was all about.

ret intervened: "Cruit, never argue with an idiot. People watching may not be able to tell the difference."

"Downtown!" John shouted above the chant: "Eee-zy out, eee-zy out, eee-zy out."

I heard the crack of the ball.

"Oh, my God!" my father said, "that kid can hit!"

The coach stopped Chris as he slid into third.

"Nice!" John said, giving him the high sign.

Margaret was at parade rest, silent, but beaming with pride.

Chris's moment of glory was cut short when the green coach yelled, "They got lucky!"

In fact they got lucky twice, then three times, then four times. At the bottom of the ninth they were tied 5–5. The bases were loaded. Kevin got up to bat.

"Come on Kevin," John called, "out of the park!"

"You can do it, buddy," Margaret said from behind the batter's cage.

A group of parents from the green team began to congregate along the sidelines. They were holding up a banner claiming the championship.

"You mind not standing there with that banner?" Margaret said to the parents. "It's distracting Kevin and his teammates."

They ignored her.

Kevin swung and missed.

"Good eye," Margaret said.

Kevin swung again, this time making contact.

"A fly ball out to center!" John cheered as the winning run slid home.

Within seconds chaos broke out on the field. The two coaches were nose to nose. Each side claimed the championship.

"Number 20 was tagged out!" the green coached said.

"I wasn't!" Number 20 said. "My foot was on the bag!"

"Sixteen tagged you!" said the green coach.

"He was safe," argued the orange coach.

"What's all the fuss?" my mother asked. "I don't like this."

"We need Tommy Lasorda to straighten this out," my father called, trying to add levity.

Nobody laughed.

"This just isn't right," my mother said. "It's only a game."

"When we were kids playing stick ball on the street, nothing like this ever happened," my father said. "The worst thing that ever happened to any of us was getting smacked for the broken broomstick when we got back home."

"I've got it on videotape," said the guy in the Bollés. "We tagged him."

I suddenly wished that John was around. The moment the game was over, John left to catch up on his writing.

"That kid can't run worth shit," said a father in a Merrill Lynch baseball cap and plaid Bermuda shorts. "For chrissake, he was tagged out!"

The kid who was tagged out began to cry. Chris and several of his teammates went over to comfort him.

"Let's go to the videotape," said Mr. Bollé.

The green parents were cracking open bottles of Perrier and telling their kids that they won.

"Listen," the orange coach said, "Mr. Lampston was standing behind the catcher and he called it safe. So we're going to go with his call."

"You're a bunch of liars!" the green coach said.

"Hold it!" a voice called from behind the batter's cage. It was Margaret. "What's the lesson we're teaching these kids?" she asked, taking center stage. "Winning at all costs? Well, where I'm from it's not the winning but how the game is played."

There was silence. The two coaches who were nose to nose slowly eased out of each other's space. The parents put down the victory banner and the Perrier.

"I wasn't raised in this fancy town," Margaret said, "Thank God for that! Where I grew up good sportsmanship was the name of the game. The message these kids are getting is wrong. These youngsters need to be guided along a moral path. They need role models. In order to be good citizens, they have to know right from wrong. This is our country. We are one. Divided we are nothing!"

"She's all right," my father said.

I looked over at my mother. Her eyes were watery.

"Well, that's all I have to say," Margaret told a very subdued group of parents.

As Margaret walked off the field, the green coach, the orange coach and Mr. Lampston huddled. I held my breath.

"Parents and players," the green coach said, "may I have your attention! I'd like that young woman who just spoke so eloquently to please step forward."

Margaret took off her U.S.S. *Arizona* cap, tucked it underneath her arm, winked at Chris, and joined the three men.

"Margaret," the green coach said, "it took an outsider to remind us what the game of Little League is all about. We've acted like a bunch of idiots." The other two coaches nodded in agreement. "And as sure as we're standing here now, that will not be repeated next season, or any other season as long as we're coaching."

For the first time all morning, both sides cheered at the same time. The only person who didn't cheer was my mother. She was busy digging through her bag for a tissue.

Margaret came up to my mother. "Ma'am," she said, "would it be okay if Cruit and I invite both teams back to the house for hot dogs and burgers and try out the 'O' course?"

"Only if I get to help cook," my mother said, adding, "And you and Cruit can train me on your 'O' course, too."

While my father and John grilled the hot dogs and burgers, Margaret and Chris gave each kid a crash course in climbing a wall, dropping down, crawling through barrels, leaping over trenches, swinging from a rope across the river and swimming back. All during this, my mother darted in and out of the house with fresh towels, more buns, soda and chips. Every so often she'd check with Margaret to see what she should do next. At one point my mother was wearing Margaret's U.S.S. *Arizona* cap to keep the sun out of her face. It was a real Norman Rockwell picture. I wanted the day to last forever.

CHAPTER 10

In the summer of 1985, four years before Margaret moved in, the most incredible thing happened to me. Bette Davis came to my house for dinner and ended up staying for an entire month.

It all began in the A & P, in Westport, Connecticut. I ran into an old friend of mine, Robin Brown. One thing led to another, and I told her that later on John and I were going to throw some chicken on the grill, and I said, "Why don't you come over?"

Robin told me that she had a houseguest. Then she told me who her houseguest was: Bette Davis. They were childhood chums. Robin asked if Bette could tag along. They'd bring a covered dish.

So, I was in the middle of the produce aisle, sandwiched between the seedless grapes and Chiquita bananas, in a state of profound shock. Bette Davis tagging along to my house? With a covered dish? I had been a devoted fan since I was a young girl growing up in Cleveland. My grandmother and I used to write her fan letters asking for her autograph and photo. I had quite a collection until Sister Mary Agnes—the one who nicknamed me "Dupa"—confiscated the wad. She replaced them with a holy card of St. Bernice, patron saint of poverty.

"Dupa," said Sister Mary Agnes, "pray to St. Bernice every

day. She will take from you away your shame desires from your filthy mind for pleasures of the world."

"I shall pray away my shame desires from my filthy mind," I said, in my slight Polish accent.

At seven o'clock that night, the doorbell rang. There was Bette Davis, the First Lady of the Silver Screen, standing on my doorstep, holding a pot of baked beans in one hand and a cigarette in the other.

Through the cigarette smoke, I could smell the molasses and bacon. My first words to Bette Davis were: "I love baked beans!" Her first words to me were: "Rips the fat right out of you!"

"They're Bette's special recipe," Robin said.

Christopher was hiding behind my jean skirt, "Who's that lady with the scary eyes, Mom?" he whispered.

"Never mind," I said, to four-year-old Christopher. "Run along and help Sun Lee pack her bags."

Sun Lee was Nanny Number Eight. She was leaving the following morning to go live in a commune somewhere in upstate New York.

Halfway into the dinner, I got up the courage to speak. "Miss Davis, I read somewhere that one of your favorite lines is from *All About Eve* when Margo turns to her guests and says: 'Fasten your seat belts—it's going to be a bumpy flight!'"

Before I even had a chance to regret opening my mouth, she attacked with all the venom and fire of Margo Channing herself.

"Keee-ryst! You and everyone else have that line wrong!" she spouted in her staccato speech. Her eyes were popped like ping-pong balls.

"Margo said, 'Fasten your seat belts—it's going to be a bumpy night!'"

John came to my rescue. "Liz, what was that other line I've heard you quote so often?"

"Oh," I said, thinking here was my chance to get back into her good graces. "It was from your movie, *Now, Voyager*, Miss Davis. Charlotte turns to Jim and says, 'Oh Jim, let's not ask for the moon when we have the stars.'"

"Jim?" Bette roared. "Who the fuck is Jim? It was *Jerry!* Charlotte turned to Jerry and said, 'Oh Jerry, let's not ask for the moon when we have the stars.'"

Devastated I excused myself and went into the kitchen. John followed.

"I'm really scared to go back."

"She's got a serious controlling disorder," John said, dragging on his pipe.

"We'd better get the dessert out," I whispered.

"Yeah, and send Mother Teresa on her merry way."

"She's so touchy," I said.

"For chrissake, Liz, it was 'Jerry' not 'Jim.' Or was it Jim? No it was Jerry. Let's go ask her."

"You're not funny," I said. "Do me a favor, go upstairs and make sure Sun Lee doesn't let Chris come down. I'm afraid he's going to comment on her eyes again."

"I'm afraid she's going to set him on fire with that cigarette. She twirls those things like a propeller on an old Piper Cub."

Shortly after dessert, she sank her cigarette into what was left of her pie, swept up her Chanel handbag, and said in clipped, curt Bette Davis: "Thank you for a most pleasant dinner. The blueberry pie was delicious."

She lit a fresh cigarette, took an inhuman drag, and said, "The chicken was so raw it nearly pecked me!"

I was convinced we had given her salmonella. But just before she left, she asked to see the rest of the house. She said that there was nothing she admired more than New England charm.

I immediately showed her our studio offices. I figured that that might give us some credibility. She appeared interested. She even asked a few questions about the kinds of books we wrote.

She told us that she was writing a book too. But she couldn't concentrate at the Ritz-Carlton in New York because of the fire trucks and sirens. "You are *most* fortunate to be able to work in such a serene and tranquil environment." Then her eyes darted around the room. "How enchanting," she said. "Does a charming cottage like this have a guest room?"

I told her that it did. For the first time all evening she seemed pleased.

The very next day the phone rang. "Darling," she said, "I've nevvvvver in my life asked *anyone* this before, but I'm in a real bind. There's a hotel strike going on in New York. In the middle of the night, Robin was called to an emergency in Maine. I was wondering if I could stay with you and John for a night— possibly two?"

Before she hung up she said, "A firm mattress is always a treat."

Less than twenty-four hours later, a stretch limo pulled into our potholed driveway. It was followed by a station wagon carrying eighteen pieces of Mark Cross luggage.

While John and the chauffeur were filing in with the bags, Sun Lee and a fella with a long gray ponytail and karate outfit were filing out with Sun Lee's belongings, loading them into a beat-up van airbrushed with a scene of the Rocky Mountains. The van and the shiny stretch limo were side by side.

"Sun Lee," I said, "I'd like you to meet Ms. Bette Davis."

Sun Lee, pressed the palms of her hands together Indian-style, bowed her head, and said, "Namaste."

Bette blew a gigantic smoke ring and walked into the guest room. "Broooother, now I've seen it all," I heard her say.

Sun Lee had moved in on the evening of the full moon, a major clue. Before her prayer rug was rolled out, Sun Lee established herself as a gifted visionary who was simply buying time as a nanny until she was recognized as the greatest prophet the world has ever known.

Sun Lee spoke with an East Indian accent, although she was from Omaha. Her real name was Sally Cook. She was given the name "Sun Lee" by a guru who had his own half-hour radio show out of Sedona, Arizona—a very sacred place, I was told.

Sun Lee's days off and many of her *not* days off were spent at a Buddhist monastery in New York State. It was at this retreat that she learned to hone her fine senses, extending them far beyond that of the ordinary mortal. To pay for this divine gift, Sun Lee did what was called "sava." This was Buddhist Jargon for KP duty. Sun Lee did *not* do "sava" outside a religious environment, a fact that burned John.

In fact, Sun Lee would return from the monastery so exhausted from doing "sava" that she would have to take to her bed for rest and meditation, cleansing her body and soul. Chris was not permitted to knock on her door if he heard harp and flute tapes—or if he smelled incense.

Sun Lee's room looked like a cave. There were crystals everywhere. One evening, while we were out, Christopher leaped off her bed, slicing his foot on an "amethyst point" that was used to heal emotional wounds.

Sun Lee treated the cut with the essence of wild rose and cherry plum.

"The drops cure," Sun Lee said with a dramatically thicker Indian accent, "not by healing the wound, but by flooding the body with the beautiful vibrations of our Higher Nature."

"What the hell is she talking about?" John said, as he swabbed the cut with Bactine.

Sun Lee was a master at asking unanswerable questions with the intent of stimulating intellectual thought and discussion—something she picked up at the monastery.

For example, she would ask: "If a child cries and nobody hears, what was the child's need?"

Soon Chris began asking imponderable questions at preschool, practically driving his teacher to an early retirement. "If we have a fire drill," Chris asked, "and all the kids are at the sandbox, do we still have a fire drill?"

Confused, his teacher answered, "No, Chris, because there's nobody in the classroom to have the drill."

"Then what is the purpose of the drill?" Chris asked.

"To get all the children out in case of a fire," his teacher said.
"Weren't all the children already out?" Chris persisted.

John posed his own imponderable question. "Sun Lee," he asked, "if a family hires a nanny to look after their child, and the nanny is frequently absent, what is the purpose of a nanny?"

Sun Lee had a thousand-mile-stare. Then she answered in a still thicker Indian accent: "True absence is one of the appointed paths to attainment."

At that point, John suggested that Sun Lee put in a forty-hour work-week or pack up her prayer rug and crystals and hit the Divine Road back to Omaha.

Shortly after the ultimatum, Sun Lee gave notice. But we weren't quite sure it was notice until we read the last line of the note.

"There is no knowledge, no ignorance, no samskara, no vijnana, no namarupa, no sadayantana, no sparsa, no vedana, no trishna and no old age and death. You owe me two weeks severence pay."

Within hours of moving into the guest room, Bette Davis proclaimed that Christopher was in dire need of discipline, proper English and proper attire.

"Mary Pop-Eyes is here to save the day," John hissed when he overheard Bette chastising Chris, "Young man, I shall not have you coming into *my* room without knocking! And, for heaven's sake, what is all that red stuff dripping down your shirt?"

"Skabetty," Christopher said.

"Whatttt-is-ska-betty?"

"Oh, that's what he calls spaghetti," I explained.

"Young man, repeat after me: spa-get-ti."

"Spa-get-ti," he said to Bette Davis's applause.

"I nevvvver believe in allowing a child to speak baby talk," Bette said. She flung a lit match into the fireplace, and ordered: "Now scoot off to your room. Your mother and I need to plan dinner." Then Bette pivoted toward me and asked, "Where's that odd blonde girl with the strange accent who was looking after him?"

"That was Sun Lee," I said. "She moved out this morning. She didn't really work out all that great."

"Deliver me from nannies!" Bette said, pouring herself a vodka and orange juice to mark the cocktail hour.

I was frantically trying to recall what Robin had said about the dos and don'ts of conversation. We weren't supposed to discuss the obvious, like, "Gee, Miss Davis, it looks like rain today," or "What a lovely sunny day." She abhorred small talk. In addition, we weren't to ask her about her health, former marriages, movies that bombed, and coactors—at the top of the list was Joan Crawford.

I took my chances and said, "I haven't had much luck with nannies."

God, I sounded so stupid.

She pursed her lips and shifted those bulbous eyes toward me. A deadly silence descended upon the room.

I was wallowing in my stupidity when Bette erupted: "That goddam Sherry took off with the nursemaid. Jeeee-sus, I'm at the studio all day working myself to deatttth. And Sherry, that bastard, is home screeeewing the nanny. And I paid him alimony. Ha! It was worth every penny of it to get riddddd of him!" she said, stabbing her cigarette into Christopher's plastic tow truck.

I couldn't believe my eyes. Sizzling plastic. I couldn't believe my ears. Bette Davis had just confided that her third husband, William Sherry, took off with the nanny. Maybe I should confide something personal about my life to keep the ball rolling.

"Boy, there are times when I think that it would really be great to live alone. Men can be such jerks."

"It's hellll living alone!"

This was all moving too fast for me.

"It's much better to be in a healthy relationship," I said.

"For Christ's sake, make up your goddamned mind," she said.

NANNIES

She seemed to like those expletives. I'd try speaking her language.

"If I caught my husband screwing a goddamn nanny I'd break his fucking back for chrissake!"

Bette turned to me with wide and pleased eyes. "Let's have scallops for dinner."

"I love scallops. I'll pick some up now."

"Ducky," Bette said. "And darling, remind me that I have a hair appointment on Friday."

Friday? Today was only Tuesday. What happened to the one or possibly two days she said over the phone? How was I going to break this news to John? It was not going to be a pretty scene.

On the morning of Day Fourteen Bette announced: "Darling, ever since I've been here you've been working your fingers to the bone. I'd like to take you and John out for dinner tonight."

"What fun," I said, planning in my head what I'd wear. Bette had once commented that I looked good in black.

Our reservations were for seven. The babysitter arrived at a quarter to. Christopher greeted her at the door in his new clipped, curt Bette Davis: "I-hope-you-know-how-to-play-Candy-Land-for-chrissake!"

John seized on that. It was a good thing Bette was still in her room getting ready.

"Nothing is worse than a four-year-old clone of Bette Davis," he said as he grabbed the car keys. Then he looked me up and down and added, "What's with the black party dress?"

"Sometimes a woman has to get dressed up to feel like somebody!" I snapped.

"I like you in denim, Liz."

"Keee-ryst!" I exploded, "I'm sick to my stomach of walking around looking like the help. I'm nothing but a goddam maid!"

"I see you've been getting acting lessons in the guest room," he said.

The afternoon of Day Twenty-one, I got out of the car with

Bette and Christopher at Compo Beach. Bette was incognito in a large straw hat, sunglasses, white duck slacks and *my* beach sandals. Christopher scooted ahead with his bucket and shovel.

Bette picked her way around the crowd to the edge of the water where Christopher had already joined a cluster of kids erecting a sand castle.

"Where would you like me to put the beach chairs?" I asked.

"On the damned beach."

"Right." I promptly unfolded her chair.

"I hope we're on the *Smoking* side of the beach!" Bette said, cupping her hand to light a cigarette.

We were settled in our chairs for only a short time before a fight broke out at the sand castle.

"Christopher!" Bette called.

"Yes, Bette Davis," Christopher said. Christopher always called her by her full name. Bette appeared to enjoy that.

"Bette Davis is not going to sit here and hear screeching children who cannot get along. If that behavior continues we shall pack up and leave. Did you hear me, young man?"

"Yes, Bette Davis," Christopher said, according her total respect.

Moments later, Bette said, "Liz darling would you mind bringing me some water. I need to take my pills."

As I walked to the sandwich shop, I wanted to shout to everyone that I was hanging out with Bette Davis! Bette Davis was wearing my beach sandals. Baby-sitting my kid. Bette Davis was even taking my phone messages.

Earlier in the day, while I was having a shower, Bette answered the phone:

"Elizabeth," Bette said with all the formality of an executive secretary, "Christopher's pediatrician's office phoned. First the nurse said, 'We need to change the time of Christopher's appointment tomorrow from two o'clock to three.' Then she called right back and said, 'No, keep it at two o'clock.' And I told her: 'Make up your goddamned mind.'"

It took nearly fifteen minutes in line to get Bette's cup of water. When I arrived back at our beach chairs, Christopher wasn't there.

"Where's Christopher?"

Bette looked up from her newspaper and said, "I thought he was with you?"

"Oh, no, maybe he's in the water!"

"Has anybody seen a little boy in a red bathing suit?" I called to everybody.

People rose from their chairs and towels and began searching with me.

"Somebody get a lifeguard!" hollered a husky man, dripping in oil. "A little boy's missing!"

There is no fear that equals that of losing your child. I suddenly thought back to an incident that happened when I was thirteen. It was the dog days of August. My brother and I were in the backyard. My best friend, Linda, biked to my house.

"Bobby's missing!" she said, leaping off her Schwinn. "Have you seen him?"

It's strange how the mind allows you to remember specific details, trivia, during highly emotional times. That day, I was wearing my yellow polka dot bathing suit. Everybody had one after that song: "Itsy-bitsy, teeny-weeny, yellow polka dot bikini." Gary and I were eating cherry popsicles and exploding caps with rocks. The sprinkler was on. We had been running through it. My mother was watering my grandfather's vegetable garden. She was wearing a bathing cap with rubber flowers.

"Nope," I said. "I haven't seen him. Maybe he's at Lawrence's?"

"I already checked," Linda said. "He's wandered off somewhere."

"Maybe old cootie-face gave him a ride on the ice cream truck?" my brother said.

Bobby was Linda's seven-year-old brother. Linda's mother worked every day, leaving Bobby in Linda's care during summer vacation. Linda's father had died from a sudden heart attack the year before. Bobby was always with us. He was our little mascot. He didn't lack for attention from the teenagers. We'd give him piggyback rides, swing him around like an airplane and spend countless hours tossing balls to him. We all believed that one day he'd be one of the Cleveland Indians. He believed it too. He lived in his Cleveland Indians baseball cap.

When Linda and I wanted our privacy to talk about boys, we'd take Bobby to Walgreen's soda fountain and buy him off with a cherry coke and a pretzel stick. While he sat up on the stool, chatting with Mrs. Kruger, we'd read the movie magazines and use the pay telephone.

The neighbors formed a search party. My mother and brother got into the Buick. Ralphie Preuss got on his motor scooter. Linda and I scouted the neighborhood on bikes. Meanwhile, Lawrence's mother called Linda's mother home from the hospital where she worked as a nurse's aid.

At sunset we congregated at Linda's house. By this time the entire Cleveland Heights police department was searching for the towhead wearing brown shorts, a striped T-shirt and Red Ball Jets on his feet.

"Do you girls remember any strange-looking people who seemed interested in Bobby?" the police asked. "Where did he play? Who are his friends?" The questions were endless.

We racked our brains. Linda's small bungalow was filled with neighbors and relatives. Everybody was trying to be optimistic. "That little devil's probably sound asleep at a new friend's house . . . By morning we'll be laughing about all of this . . . From now on, he's never to be left alone for even one minute . . ."

At ten o'clock that night, the police returned. One of the officers was holding the Cleveland Indians baseball cap. They took Linda's mother into the kitchen and closed the door. It was very quiet. Then we heard a scream. This was followed by sobbing. Bobby had been found floating face down in the Wilsons' pond.

I ran along the edge of the water with macabre images of Christopher floating face down.

"We need a lifeguard!" insisted the man dripping in coconut oil.

"Christopher!" I shouted, imagining the worst.

A mother came up to me carrying an infant. She said that five minutes earlier she had seen a man dragging off a little boy kicking and screaming. He may have been wearing a red bathing suit. She couldn't be sure.

At that very moment, a loud, clear voice blasted from the lifeguard's bullhorn: "I've got a boy named Christopher who wants 'Mommy and Bette Davis' to come get him."

The entire beach had heard the bullhorn and an entourage of autograph seekers followed her.

"Hi, Bette Davis," Christopher said, beaming. He was sitting on the lifeguard's lap, pleased with all the attention.

"Are you *the* Bette Davis?" the lifeguard asked.

"I *am the* Bette Davis. Just as that young man on your lap said." Bette turned her undivided attention to Christopher: "Young man, you have given us quite a scare."

Then she turned to the horde of fans coated in lotion and announced in Broadway-British: "If you will please stand in a proper line, I'll be delighted to give you my autograph."

The gaping crowd did as the movie star requested.

The lifeguard cleared a small area on his desk and for the next twenty minutes Bette signed autographs on damp napkins.

On the way home, Bette blasted Paul Newman for not extending the same courtesy to the fans who paid for his success.

"You know Miss Davis," I said, "I know Paul Newman has a policy of never giving his autograph, but he's donated millions of dollars to worthwhile charities from the profits of his salad dressing and spaghetti sauce."

Bette flicked her cigarette out the window: "Big fucking deal!"

Christopher said from his carseat: "Mommy, Bette Davis just said the 'F' word."

"Christopher," I said, "mind your own business."

Elizabeth Fuller

"Christopher is absolutely correct. I shall not use any more 'F' words in front of little ears."

A millisecond later she said, "Shit, every time I think of how Newman refuuused to sign autographs, I want to vaaaaahmit!"

When we arrived back home, Sun Lee was sitting cross-legged on our front stoop. She had a mutt at her side.

"Sun Lee?" I said, as Bette stormed past, "What happened?"

Sun Lee broke down in tears. Then she detailed why she split from the monastery.

From what I gathered it was a full day of "sava," grinding flour, plucking grapes, wheat, weeds, cleaning the dorms and sending out mailings. The day ended with Sun Lee spinning the prayer wheel.

"Prayer wheel?" I asked.

"Sending mantras out to the universe for the starving sister monastery in Mill Valley," she said without a trace of her Indian accent.

Christopher plopped his empty sand pail on top of the scrawny mutt's head. "What's your doggy's name?" he asked

"Tao," Sun Lee said. "He almost died from eating bad tofu. He was the only one I could relate to at Sing Sing."

"What about the fella who helped you move out of here?" I asked. "You seemed to like him quite a bit."

"Duhkha's on his way to Mill Valley to franchise Sila workshops," Sun Lee said. He dropped me off on his way. Her eyes welled. He said I couldn't go along. I need to work on my 'Samudaya'—evil karma."

"What on earth is a Sila workshop?"

"Ten-week courses to do away with the sexual impulse," Sun Lee said, not the least bit annoyed at my total ignorance.

"Oh," I said. "And what does the name 'Duhkha' mean?"

"It means, 'life is suffering,'" she said, living proof.

"You must be hungry," I said. "Come on in."

"Namaste," she said.

CHAPTER 11

THE FOLLOWING MORNING I found John leafing through the New York *Times* searching for news of the hotel strike.

"Hi, darling," I said, "where's Bette?"

"Liz," John said, "I won't go through another evening like we had last night! We're caught between the jaws of the sacred and the profane."

"Not to worry," I said, "Sun Lee just told me that she's leaving tomorrow for Omaha."

"Thank God for small favors. That mangy dog goes too?"

"Of course," I said. "But she needs to borrow two hundred dollars for a ticket."

"What?"

"She's flat broke," I said.

"We gave her two weeks' severance pay for Christ's sake!"

"When she checked into the monastery she had to give up all of her worldly goods."

"Well, she's not getting any more worldly goods from us. Case closed."

"If we don't give her the money, she won't leave."

"She's gotta leave," John said. "This is our house."

"We can't throw her out with no place to go."

John helped himself to the remains of the coffee and softened. "Why can't her parents wire her the money?"

"Bad crop season," I said.

"Liz, I want a note from her that she'll pay us back. Every penny."

"Then you'll give her the money?"

"Make sure she catches the first flight out of here. Another night like . . ."

I felt that John had overreacted to the dinner the night before. Personally, I think the bugs and humidity got to him more than Sun Lee and Bette.

It was muggy and hot. We don't have air conditioning so I suggested to Bette that we have a picnic down at the river.

"A spleeendid idea," Bette said. "I shall make my baked beans. Do we have Colman's dry mustard?"

"I'll run to the store," I said.

"And darling, while you're there, I'll need a carton of Vantage, the *Daily News* and Carnation Instant Breakfast drink— chocolate flavored."

"I can't forget the chicken either," I said, wondering if she were going to give me any money. She didn't. "I'll have John grill it."

"For God's sake make sure he cooks it this time."

The evening went downhill when Sun Lee tried to revive a spider Bette swatted off the table. To make matters worse, Sun Lee, wrapped in an Indian bedspread, insisted on leading us in a mantra before we broke the pita: "Om mani padme hummmmmm," she chanted, insensitive to her audience.

"That means the jewel in the eye of the lotus," Sun Lee told the chillingly mute Bette Davis.

"Christopher, put that spider down!" John commanded.

"Envelope him in healing white light," Sun Lee told Chris.

"Jeeee-sus," Bette said.

"So, Bette," John said, "any news on when they're going to shoot the movie in Italy?"

"I phoned Rome again this afternoon," Bette said, tossing a lit cigarette into the dry woods. "It's expected to come through at any time."

"I hope she's putting those calls on her credit card," John said when he got up to flip the chicken.

When Bette Davis was our houseguest she was wonderful with
Chris, even consulting with him about what to color
Mickey Mouse's ears.

"Sun Lee," I said, "help yourself to some of Miss Davis's baked beans."

"Is there anything that had once lived in them?" Sun Lee asked.

Bette raised her half-moon eyebrows.

"Sun Lee's a strict vegetarian," I said, trying to smooth things over. "I think she wants to know if there's any pork in them."

"Or pork flavoring," Sun Lee said, setting strict guidelines.

"Of course, there's pork in them," Bette growled. "How in the hell do you make proper baked beans without pork?"

"My religion does not allow me to eat anything that has been killed," Sun Lee said.

"Broooother," said Bette.

"Broooother," said Chris.

"Sun Lee," I said, "go in the house and make yourself some rice."

"I shall fast," said the holy young woman, dropping her eyelids and folding her hands, Gandhi-style.

"Young lady," Bette said, taking control, "your behavior is rude and unforgiving. You are *our* guest for dinner."

John muttered: *"our* guest?"

Sun Lee reluctantly helped herself to some salad even though the dressing was made with anchovies. She passed on the beans and chicken.

"Miss Davis is waiting for a role to come through in Italy," I said, breaking the awkward silence.

Sun Lee asked: "Have you ever acted in the United States?"

Bette's eyes almost left their orbits.

"Miss Davis is one of the most famous movie stars who has ever lived," I said. "She's known all over the world. In fact she's even bigger in England than she is here."

"So was Bloody Mary," John said, ready for a shoot-out at the O.K. Corral.

"Mr. Fuller," Bette retorted, "you'd be the *first* I'd behead."

"What does 'behead' mean, Bette Davis?" Chris asked.

Bette Davis did not answer. Sun Lee got on her soapbox: "It's what they do to cattle at the slaughterhouses."

"Jeeee-sus," Bette said, "that woman is obsessed with dead animals."

"I have no obsession," Sun Lee said. "I have no knowledge, no ignorance, no samskara, no vijnana, no . . ."

"We know all that," John said. "Sun Lee, *what* are your plans?"

"I must be obedient to karma," she said, fingering the rose quartz that hung from one ear lobe.

"I think what John meant was, are you going to contact Mrs. Hollenbeck to seek another nanny position?"

Sun Lee stared off into the woods. Then she said, "All things are empty. There is nothing desirable to seek in the material world."

Bette looked as if she were on the verge of a major explosion. It took Sun Lee's next words to trigger it.

Sun Lee turned her painted blue eyes toward Bette. Then accidentally slipping into a Nebraska twang, she asked: "Do you know Shirley MacLaine?"

Vesuvius erupted: "Gawd, if I hear that woman on one more talk show drooling over her past lives, I'm going to—"

"Vaaaaahmit!" Chris said.

"Liz," John said as we got ready for bed, "we're losing control of our house—our lives—our integrity—our *child* for God's sake!"

"You're blowing it out of proportion."

"You may enjoy having your idol camped here, running up the phone bill, grocery bill and everything else, but I'm not! Chris is suffering."

"That's not true," I said. "Bette's so good with Chris. Just today Christopher went to her room with his crayons and said, 'Bette Davis will you color with me?' I overheard her asking Chris's advice on what color to crayon Mickey's ears. He said, 'Bette Davis, you stay in the lines real good.'"

John did not want to hear about the good.

"Liz, you heard him tonight, mimicking her every word."

"That was cute," I said.

"Cute? A few minutes ago when I went to his room and said,

'Give Daddy a kiss goodnight,' he bugged out those little eyes and snapped, 'What for?' And I said, 'Because daddy loves you.' And he flailed his arm—just like you know who—and said, 'Such-a-pity.'"

"I'm sure the hotel strike will be over any day now."

"She's got three days to pack her bags," John said. "If she's not out of here by Saturday morning, *I'm* out of here."

On the evening of Day Twenty-eight, one day before John's Davis Departure Deadline, D-Day, Bette was settled down at her favorite nook with her nightly glass of wine. Christopher was curled up next to her watching Mister Rogers, and as Bette said: "His visit to a goddam marble factory." John was hunched at the kitchen bar, checking the AT&T overseas calls and other bills. I was in the kitchen preparing supper.

"Liz," John said, "what is this vet charge? We don't have a dog."

I dreaded this moment.

"Tao needed some shots," I said.

"Who?"

"You know, Sun Lee's dog."

"It's a hundred-and-seventy-five-dollar bill!"

"He really needed those shots," I said.

"Let me get this straight," John said. "This bill is in addition to the two-hundred for the airline ticket?"

"She promised to pay us back," I said. "She even wanted to give me her gold topaz as collateral. It's for joy."

"Did Holly ever pay us anything for Mr. Unger's vet bill?"

Christopher, hearing Mr. Unger's name, sang: "When you're driving in your Chevy and you're feeling a little heavy, diarrhea, diarrhea . . ."

"Enough of that, Christopher!" I called.

Bette's eyes were glued to the world of Mister Rogers.

"Something's wrong with a man who takes off his sneakers on television!" Bette said.

"Bette Davis," Christopher said, "that makes me want to vaaaahmit!"

"What a creep!" Bette said.

"What-a-creep!" Chris said about the man he watched every day of his life.

Day Twenty-nine: I woke up and realized that it was John's Davis Departure Deadline. His car was gone. He must have been serious about leaving.

Bette was in the kitchen sipping her breakfast drink and reading the newspaper, oblivious to the fact that I was now a single parent.

"Liz, darling," Bette said, handing me a shopping list, "we're out of cream and mayo."

I was just getting used to the idea that I'd be living in this little cottage on the river with just my son and Bette Davis for the rest of my life when I heard John's old Audi pull into the driveway.

He presented me with my favorite flower—a pink rose. There was a note attached to it. It read: "Liz, if you should ever question my love, remember this summer of '85."

He also gave me a Penguin paperback of *Macbeth*. On Lady Macbeth he had drawn pop eyes and a cigarette.

Day thirty-two: Bette burst into the kitchen and announced: "The hotel strike is over! The limo will be here at ten o'clock tomorrow morning."

The morning of her departure, Bette went into Chris's room to say goodbye.

"Young man," Bette said, slipping on her white gloves, "I want to thank you for letting Bette Davis share your lovely house. We had a lot of good times together. I shall miss you. And I hope you never forget the rules to the What a Dump Game we invented.

"I won't, Bette Davis," Chris said, "When you coming back?"

Bette answered his question with a question.

"How would you like Bette Davis to leave her number with your mother and father? You may phone me from time to time. We'll have a nice chat all about Superman."

"Are you going to see Superman?"

"Perhaps in the studio commissary," Bette said, running her gloved hand through his hair. "Remember, it's all pretend. Superman can't really fly. So I don't want you to be leaping off the sofa anymore. You were lucky last time."

"Will you send me a big picture of you, Bette Davis?"

I had to smile thinking that we might have another Bette Davis fan in the works. Even John grinned at that one.

Then Bette turned to me, lowered her voice, and said, "With a bit more discipline, he will grow into a handsome, charming young man. Children need rules. Be firm. Christopher would do well being dressed properly. I shall send him something from Italy."

I nodded and then we hugged goodbye.

"Oh, and Elizabeth," Bette said moments before she stepped into the limo, "you are most fortunate to have both a bright, attractive son and husband. John is opinionated, determined and gutsy—all the ingredients to make him a first-rate husband. The world is loaded with spineless sissies. Keep a close eye on him."

I went back into the house to find two little poems in her handwriting:

Never again say "yes"
to any request to
stay with you
During a strike,
As you now know,
It is possible for
~~this guest~~
To stay for life!!
        Much love
        "always"
Chris's "Bette Davis"
Give him a hug
And a kiss for
    me.

As I sit here and wait
To drive away
Not in a one horse
        ~~open~~ sleigh.
Please do not feel
        dismay,
If you want to clap
        your hands
            with glee,
Because you will see no
        more of me !!

B. D.

CHAPTER 12

BETTE DAVIS BLITZED the burbs over four years ago. Now, after a long Memorial Day weekend, Margaret, my mother and I were sitting around the kitchen table listening to Chris explain how to play the What a Dump game.

"You take this cigarette," Chris said, "and place it in the center of the table. Close your eyes. Spin it, and then you try and guess which direction it's pointing, like north, south, east or west. The first person to guess correctly is the winner."

My folks were preparing to head back home, after a visit chock full of surprises—all pleasant ones. Who could have predicted that my mother, Margaret and I would stay up past midnight each night, chatting away about everything from German U-boats to very personal issues Margaret had never discussed with anyone, ever?

"The last time I saw my mother," Margaret confided, "I was six years old. I remember her holdin' my hand and taking me to an airshow. We were based at Camp Pendleton. I was mighty proud. She was beautiful. She had long brown hair that hung in loose curls. She used to pull the sides back with clips in the shape of butterflies. Dad brought them back from Japan. That day, we were both wearin' flowered sundresses. I remember asking her as we walked if she thought I'd look like her when I grew up. 'You're goin' to be prettier,' she said. I used to wait for my red hair to turn dark brown," Margaret said, forcing a laugh. "I always felt it was my fault that she left. All during growin' up, I felt that maybe I could have prevented her from leavin'."

I was proud of the way my own mother just listened, allowing Margaret to get it all out.

"Dad never wanted to talk much about her," Margaret continued. "At first, he told us that she went away to visit her sister in North Carolina. Then, one day, he came home and told us that she couldn't come back. He didn't tell us why. That was the saddest I'd ever seen Dad. My brother Bill told me that Mom had another man. I'd go to bed at night and say to myself if I could count to one million that when I got to a million and one, she'd come back."

"Margaret," my mother finally said, "have you tried to contact her?"

Margaret shook her head. "Nope."

"Maybe you should," I said.

She shrugged her shoulders.

"Margaret," my mother said, wrapping her arms around her, "I'd be proud to have you as a daughter. You're a very capable and bright young lady. I just know your mother will feel the same way. Don't be too hard on her for leaving. She *must* have had her reasons."

Margaret came to no decision that evening. But the next morning, she said that she would try to contact her mother. She thought her father might know her whereabouts.

"I'm not so sure how Dad's going to accept all of this," Margaret said as she fried eggs and cooked up a pot of grits for my parents' send-off breakfast.

"From what you've told us Margaret," my mother said, "he sounds like a reasonable man."

"Dad raised us to be strong."

"Margaret," I said, "wanting to find your mother is not a sign of weakness."

"There's the chance that she won't want to see me."

My mother and I exchanged side glances. There was that distinct possibility.

"I'm ready to take that chance," Margaret said. There was doubt in her voice. "Dad always used to say to us, 'Never ask a question, if you can't live with the answer.'"

With that, Margaret turned her attention to Christopher as he came bounding into the kitchen.

"Cruit, the good news is there's shore leave. The bad news. No boats."

"Ah, what'd I do, Sarge?"

"Fatigues on the deck of the latrine. Wet towel on the hatch."

"You're pickin' fly shit out of pepper, Sarge," Chris said, stealing Margaret's line.

"I get my orders. You get yours."

"What did he do?" my mother asked.

"He left his dirty clothes on the bathroom floor, and a wet towel on the door, Mom."

"Cruit," my mother said. "Go clean up the latrine."

"Sarge, can we still have our all-out effort to retake Guadalcanal?" Chris asked.

"Debrief at 1100," Margaret said, reaching for the phone. It was Janet. She needed to talk to me at once.

All hell had broken loose. Howard found out about Janet's affair with Danny. Janet suspected that Helga was the informer. Howard went crazy. At midnight, he called Janet's mother and told her that her daughter was a nympho. Then at one o'clock he called her again and said that he wanted to have her committed to a mental institution for the "sexually insane." At four, he called for the third time and said that he was going to take the children and file for divorce. When Janet tried to get the Princess phone away from him, he cracked her on the head with the receiver. He hit her so hard that call waiting doesn't work. Janet's a basketcase. Danny's on the road. His beeper isn't turned on. He could show up at Janet's anytime now. Howard stayed home from the office to keep watch on her. Janet gave me Danny's beeper number. Could I please try the number until I get him?

"Janet," I said, "where's Howard now?"

"In the shower," she said, barely audible. "He's got the cellular phone. I can't talk." Click.

When I told my mother she said, "If that isn't Nunzio all over again."

"You mean Nunzio found out about Aunt Rosie and Uncle Rocco?"

"He called a family meeting," my mother said. "Your grandmother went to it. All the relatives were invited. Of course your father and I wouldn't go. How he humiliated Aunt Rosie. He never touched her after that. He said she was a diseased woman."

"Oh, my God," I said. "After everything he had done?"

"Same as Howard," my mother said, smoothing fresh sheets on her bed.

"My heart goes out to Aunt Rosie," I said.

"God bless her," my mother said. "And now the poor thing doesn't know where she is or who she is."

"You mentioned that, Mom."

Several weeks later Margaret told me that Howard and Helga were *definitely* yodeling in the same bed together. Helga told Darlene and Darlene told Margaret. Then Darlene told Janet.

This was all too much like a French farce.

"Howard's schtuping the swensker," Janet said when I bumped into her at the Pasta Patio. She was selecting a picnic lunch for two.

I pretended I was hearing it for the first time. "Are you serious?" I said. "What are you going to do?"

"I already did it," Janet said, preoccupied with the menu. "Angelo, how does Soave Bolla go with angel hair and basil?"

"Primo!" he said, smacking his lips. "Oh, la, la, my bella's going to have a very sexy lunch and I hope a . . ."

"Angelo!" Janet said, giggling.

While Angelo bolted out, "I Love, I Love, I Love, My Little Calendar Girl" from the kitchen, Janet said that she threw Howard out. "He's living at his office and taking showers at the Y. Helga's staying there too. He put her to work yodeling to the kids. She has them sing: 'Little old lady who' five times real fast to distract them from their tightened braces."

We both laughed.

"So everything's okay with you and Danny?"

"My lawyer told me I have to be *really* careful." She grabbed a pack of matches from the counter. "For the candles," she said whisking off with the Pier Imports picnic basket brushing against Ralph Lauren baggies.

For a split second I envied her tumultuous life. And the Ann Taylor sandals. While she was off to see her lover, I was off to have the oil changed. When I returned home I had an adrenaline rush.

"Liz," John said, greeting me in the driveway, "what do you know about Marian Kibble?"

"Mrs. Kibble? Poor Mrs. Kibble?"

"The FBI was just here," John said. "They had a stack of my old manuscript papers that she had sent to the Russian embassy."

"Oh, no. Is she still sending them stuff?"

"She's taken an alias as John G. Fuller," John said. He was fuming.

"Oh, no!"

"I told them that her sneakers aren't laced all the way to the top," John said. "I don't think they'll be back."

"I guess that medication isn't working too well."

"Apparently not," John said. "Good thing we have the driveway lined with American flags."

"Where're Margaret and Chris?"

"In the river, stalking German U-boats," John said. Incidentally, Margaret's been looking for you all morning. Her father's written her a letter about how to contact her mother."

"Did she show it to you?"

John nodded. "I hope it all works out for her," he said. I could see the concern in his eyes.

Dear Margaret:

The last contact I had with your mother was over ten years ago. At that time she was remarried and living in Pensacola, Florida. She is married to a Naval officer by the name of Henry

T. Palmer. I'm sure you can get the number through information. More than that, I simply don't know.

Margaret, over the years, I've tried to convince her to see you and the boys. For her own reasons, she refused contact. Although I don't know what those reasons were, I'm sure it had nothing to do with her love for her children, but her dislike for me. I know it must be very hard for a young girl to grow up without a mother. Please accept my apologies for denying you that important relationship.

I didn't know much about raising a daughter. I didn't know about hair bows, and party dresses, and all the things little girls like. I regret that.

Please try to understand that underneath this uniform, there's a confused man just trying to get to tomorrow.

Daughter, my heart aches for you above the boys. Perhaps this revelation is a day late and a dollar short, but whatever it's worth, I love you, and God knows I tried to do my best under the circumstances. I wish you fair weather and following winds.

Love,
Dad

Margaret, John, and I put our heads together to plot the next move.

CHAPTER 13

THERE WAS NO listing for a Henry T. Palmer. The naval station would give Margaret no information. John, the investigative journalist, suggested that Margaret would have more success if she actually went to the naval base.

"I've never had any luck getting classified information over the phone," John told her. I had to hand it to John, he was an expert at unearthing secret information. In fact a recent reviewer in the New York *Times Book Review* confirmed this, writing that "Even before passage of the Freedom of Information Act, Fuller had a facility for somehow obtaining government documents, which he incorporates in some of his books."

On John's advice, Margaret began to make arrangements for a trip to Pensacola. She would drive the Mustang.

"Margaret," John said, "that car won't get you across the George Washington Bridge."

"It does need a new clutch, sir," Margaret admitted about the car she and Chris waxed and polished every Saturday morning.

"The muffler's shot, too," John said, handing her a round trip ticket on USAir.

Margaret wouldn't hear of it.

"It's nonrefundable," John said. Then he told her something he rarely spoke of: "Margaret, when I was six years old, my father left. He left my mother, my sister and myself. I never saw him after that time. The only memory I have of him is sitting in his car while he visited his girlfriend. That was just before he left. When I got older my mother told me that he had become addicted to cocaine. He was a dentist and had easy access. He died when I was twelve. To this day, I don't even know how he died. I know the pain of growing up without a parent," John said, handing Margaret the ticket.

Margaret's eyes were as moist as John's. There seemed to be an unspoken bond between the two of them.

"I'm much obliged, sir."

Two days later, Margaret phoned us from Pensacola. She had located her mother, but she refused to see her. Heartbroken, Margaret returned with the saga of her journey.

"I got the number through naval security," Margaret said. "I explained the situation at base information. Showed them my I.D. After runnin' a security check, I was given the number. They wouldn't give me the address. I went back to Ho Jo's and called. A man answered. I asked to speak to Mrs. Palmer. She got right on. I said, 'Ma'am, this is a voice from your distant past.' There was no response. My heart was goin' a mile a minute. 'Who is this?' she asked.

"'Ma'am, this is your daughter, Margaret Stone.' She hung up. I had a Bud and called back. 'Ma'am,' I said, 'please talk to me.' I told her that I didn't want nothin' from her, except to see her. She wanted to know how I got her number. She didn't ask about my brothers, Bill or Tom. Of course, she didn't ask about Dad. During the silence, I told her that Dad had a heart attack. But he was okay. 'He never once said nothin' against you, ma'am.' I asked her if she still had those butterfly clips. She said that she couldn't talk. A man, guess it was her husband, got on and said that I'd upset her and don't ever be callin' back again. So here I am."

For the longest time nobody spoke. John stuffed and re-stuffed his pipe. I stared blankly out the sliding glass door, cursing myself for encouraging her to go in the first place.

"I say we all have a rest and go out for dinner," John said.

"Thank you, sir. But I think I'm going' to bunk down for the night."

"I thought we'd go to Sakura," John said. "They've got Japanese beer."

"I'm really beat, sir."

"Margaret," John said, "when I got older, I saw things differently. My pain gave me a certain strength."

"Thank you, sir," Margaret said. She threw her duffle bag over her shoulder and headed for her room. Then she stopped short. "Guess I *could* go for some chow and a brew."

"We'll leave at 1900," John said.

"Aye, aye, sir."

"You know, Margaret," John said, "Emerson admonished himself when he stopped grieving over the loss of a loved one. He felt emotional pain was necessary to affirm life."

"He'd never make it in the Marines, sir," Margaret said. Her voice was suddenly lighter.

"Probably not," John said, chuckling.

That night at the restaurant, John and I got Margaret laughing so hard the people at the next table were straining their ears to find out what was so funny. We were telling Margaret about some of her more colorful predecessors.

"Liz," John said, "did you ever tell Margaret about the vampire you almost brought here to take care of Chris?"

"A vampire to take care of me!" Chris squealed.

"Quiet in the ranks!" Margaret said. "Listen to the C.O.'s story."

John ordered us all another round of drinks, and I began my strange but true tale.

"I first met Sophia on a train going through the Romanian countryside. This was about three years ago. I was on an assignment for a travel magazine."

"Who was watching me?" Chris asked.

"Your dad and Ginger," I said. "Now let me tell the story. I was commissioned to do a Halloween piece on Dracula. I had written a couple of books on the paranormal. I guess they thought I could do the job. So I'm on the Eastern European railways, looking forward to burying myself in background research. I had four seats to myself. I picked up my Fodor's guides and began reading about the nearby Bran Castle and the Transylvanian haunts of Count Dracula . . ."

"Dracula sucks!" Chris said, biting on the cherry in his Coke.

"Well, a few moments after the train pulled out of the station, I became aware of a young woman who had slipped quietly into the row of seats opposite me. This new occupant was settled comfortably with her legs tucked under her. She was wearing a long, full flowered skirt. Sort of gypsy-style. What caught my attention were her eyes. They were wide, smiling, almost hypnotic."

"Mom, is this story scary?"

"Hush, Cruit," Margaret said, pulling him toward her for protection.

"I was a little surprised when the girl spoke in nearly perfect English. 'I see you are an American,' she said. 'I see you're very observant,' I answered. I asked her how she knew. She said, 'Your books. They are English. Are they not?'

"I told her that I could be British or Australian. She studied me closely for a moment and then shook her head. The girl seemed very mature and literate for her age. I took her to be about twenty. During our conversation she said that she always wanted to go to America. Since she was a little girl. I told her that she must do that sometime, and she nodded at the Romanian scenery out the window. She seemed so ethereal, I remember saying how beautiful the countryside was, and she said: 'There are many different kinds of beauty. I have seen many pictures of beauty in your country.' Then she added, 'And some ugliness too.' But the girl quickly apologized. 'No, there is ugliness here in Romania also.' That should have been my first clue. Anyway, she asked me if I were on a holiday.

"I told her that I was writing about the Carpathians for an American travel magazine. I was warned that the local people resent Americans' fascination with vampires.

"She asked me if I was going to Brasnov. 'Yes, to one of the ski resorts near there.' I said.

"'Good,' the girl said. 'I am working at the Carpathian Hotel at Poiana Brasnov. You must stay there and I can be your guide.'"

John cut in: "Only Liz could have found her very own vampire as a tour guide in Transylvania."

"Hey, you're wrecking my story," I said.

Margaret and Chris were hanging on my every word. And I wasn't exaggerating. It truly was one of the weirdest things that had ever happened to me.

I continued, "I was taken aback by the girl's cordiality. But I had planned on staying there anyway. And here was a source of local information I couldn't pass up. We exchanged names and made plans to meet that same evening."

"Did you sense anything strange about her?" Margaret asked.

"Not really. Just that she seemed rather ethereal. Otherworldly. She told me that she worked in the hotel's nursery. Taking care of the children when their parents were off skiing. If anything, I was impressed by her. But that evening . . ."

"Let's first order," John said, stopping long enough to tell the waiter we were all having shrimp tempura except Chris. He wanted the chicken teriyaki.

"So I checked into the hotel, had a shower and stopped by the nursery on my way to the dining room. I wanted to make contact with Sophia to plan for our tour the next day.

"Sophia was seated on a low child's chair. She was wearing a starched white nurse's uniform. A dozen children were at her feet and two on her lap. She was leading them in a song that sounded like "Itsy-Bitsy Spider." The children were mimicking spider movements with their tiny fingers. After several more animated songs, she lined up all the children and marched them in single file over to a long table where there were sliced apples and cheese. Not one child broke the line. There was no whining, pushing or shoving. What was most startling: no child began to eat until all were seated."

"Did she know you were there?" Margaret asked.

"I don't think so," I said. "She was fully absorbed with the children."

John turned to Margaret and said, "I'm sure she knew Liz was there. She was trying to impress her because she wanted to come here to become an au pair." Then John turned to me and said, "Didn't you tell her on the train that you had a small child and couldn't find decent help?"

"Will you let me tell the story," I said. "Let's see, where was I?"

"On your way to the mess hall," Margaret said.

"Right, I went to the dining room. It did not lack for atmosphere. It was a huge cavernous hall with rock walls. The eating utensils were pewter and the dining chairs were heavily cushioned in dark purple velvet to match the draperies. Smack out of the Addams Family. It was surprisingly full. When I arrived at midday, I didn't see a soul. The guests had apparently spent the day on the slopes. Sitting at the next table was a jovial group of Italian filmmakers who were doing a story for Italian TV on the Romanian vineyards—some of the best in the world I was told. When I asked if they were Romanian they burst out laughing. I was quickly informed that the only Romanian filmmaker to ever achieve prominence was a chap named Popescu-gop, for his cartoons at foreign film festivals."

"Liz," John said, "get to the story."

"I'm setting the stage," I said, irked at his impatience. "Thanks to the Italians I learned that the best wine to order was from the Murfatlar winery near the Black Sea. When the waiter returned with a long-stemmed glass of Pinot Noir, he handed me a sealed envelope. The note read: 'My dear Madame Fuller. As we spoke on the railway, I will meet with Madame after the dinner hour to make arrangements for tomorrow. At nine o'clock I will be in the hotel library.' It was signed: 'Respectfully yours, Miss Sophia Wallacha.'

"The note was so formal I did feel a little uncomfortable. But I reminded myself that I was in Romania, not the U.S.A., where any sort of etiquette is cause for suspicion."

Margaret nodded.

"So after dinner I carried a demitasse of Turkish coffee into the hotel library for my meeting with Sophia. 'Madame enjoyed dinner?' she asked. She was still wearing the nurse's uniform. I must admit that it did enter my mind that it would be nice to have someone as professional as Sophia to take care of Chris. "Of course," I quickly added, "this was all before you, Margaret."

Margaret gave a quick smile.

"I told Sophia that Romanian food was without doubt the tastiest I had ever had, and probably the richest, too. And she said, 'Our bodies are not made for such fat-producing foods. Do you not agree?' I told her that I couldn't agree more. 'Back home it's a constant battle to get Christopher to eat properly.'

"'Who is Christopher?' Sophia asked. She spread a map of brownish parchment paper on the table."

"Swell, Mom." Chris said, "you discussed my eating habits with a *vampire?*"

Margaret snickered.

"'This map looks ancient,' I told Sophia. 'It was copied from a map that was three hundred years old,' she said. 'Boy I couldn't get this kind of tour at the American Express office,' I said.

"'I want Madame to see and feel my country's enormous beauty and variety,' Sophia said. Her eyes remained locked to mine. The intensity made me feel somewhat uneasy. Big time clue."

"You probably gave her my picture," Chris said. "There's a vampire walking around with my kindergarten picture in her wallet."

"'I see you're very proud of your country,' I said to Sophia. 'It is strange, Madame, I have this deep love for my ancient land, yet I have this strong urge to go to the new country in the western world. To your country.'"

"She wanted to come here?" Margaret asked.

"Exactly," I said. "And do you want to know why?"

"Toooooo suuuuck myyy blooood," Chris said.

"Close," I said. "In my research, I read that if a vampire travels to another country where a different language is spoken, and is *undetected* for seven years, he or she becomes a human again. But I didn't know that at the time."

"Oh, Liz," John said, "that's a myth."

Margaret asked, "What'd you say to her when she hinted about comin' over?"

"Knowing Liz," John said, "she probably asked, 'Is business class okay?'"

"I said, 'Well, you must do that.' I was just being polite. But she wouldn't let it rest."

"'Yes,' Sophia said, her eyes lasered to mine, 'I have registered with a woman here who might arrange a way for me to do this.'

"'How do you mean?' I asked. 'There's an office here in the village,' she told me. 'They can arrange for what you call an au pair for taking care of children in a Western country. Just the way I do here in the hotel nursery. Or with a single family in a country like yours.'

"Sophia seemed to sense my uneasiness. She let it drop. 'But this is just my dream.' Those Transylvanian eyes were scorching my corneas.

"After interminable staring, she said, 'I promised to be a guide for you in my own country.' I told her that I really appreciated that. 'I think you will love the Carpathians. They are lovely even at night,' Sophia said. 'I must show them to you now.' I laughed. 'But how can we see anything at night?' Sophia didn't chuckle along. 'You can feel them,' she said. 'The night air is refreshing. The mountains glow even in the starshine. There's a bright moon tonight. It reflects the snow.'

"I told Sophia that I was going back to my room so that I'd be well rested for the following day. But she persisted. 'After such a heavy meal perhaps a little walk in the mountain air will refresh you,' she said."

"Mom," Chris said climbing on me to check for two puncture holes in my neck, "you didn't go with the vampire, did you?"

"She wouldn't take no for an answer. 'Your jacket is right

here in the check room. And so is mine,' she said. 'It's a short walk from here to my home in the village. You might meet my family for a moment.'"

Christopher was curled up next to Margaret in the booth.

"It wasn't long before we stepped into the night air. And I must admit that at first I felt stimulated and refreshed. It was a full moon. The snow glittered. The lights of the little village twinkled below. The peaks of the mountains loomed in silhouette . . ."

"Lizzy," John cut in, "for God's sake, you're in love with your own words. Tell the story."

I ignored John and went on: "We walked in silence, except for the squeaking of our heavy boots on the crusted snow. Halfway down to the village the dark forest closed in on us. 'There is so much to see, especially in the daylight, when you can see it,' she said reflectively. 'I'm afraid it's too late to find my family awake. But later perhaps. I love the nighttime. Do you not?'"

Chris put one finger over the other to form a cross. "That's what you should have done, Mom," he demonstrated.

"I didn't think that quickly. I told her that I was really tired and I wanted to go back to the hotel and crash."

"Did she take you back?" Margaret asked.

"We started back, moving down a very dark cobblestone lane where I became aware of a low stone wall beside us. Sophia stopped. She rested her elbows on the wall. Then I noticed a tiny cemetery. 'You must forgive me,' Sophia said. 'But here is where my family lies buried back to many generations. I come here because I feel their presence. But there is beauty here, even in death.'"

"Another clue," Margaret said.

"I was so spooked," I said, "that I could have sworn that hair began to grow on her forehead."

"Liz!" John said.

"You weren't there!" I snapped. Then I turned to Margaret and Chris and said, "It may have been the shadow of her bangs."

"Mom, you should have worn garlic around your neck." Chris's tiny face was scrunched with fright as he sat wrapped in Margaret's arms.

"You're right," I agreed. "When we finally got back to the hotel, she said, 'Tomorrow is my day off. I will take Madame to all the beauties of art and history nearby. But I hope you have felt the quiet, mystical beauty of the night and the mountains.'"

"How'd you get out of that one?" Margaret asked.

"I didn't," I said. "At eight o'clock the next morning she came to the hotel. She was wearing *sunglasses*. You know, they're sun-sensitive."

"Keep to the facts, Liz," John said.

"But instead of taking me to see all the art and history that she promised, she took me on a tour to a makeshift au pair agency. It was in the back of a tailor shop on the outskirts of the village. Sophia had apparently told the agency that we'd be arriving. The moment I stepped through a beaded doorway, a large woman with a faint beard, wearing several pin cushions around her wrist, motioned for me to have a seat behind one of the foot-pedal sewing machines. For a second I was afraid that she was going to throw a hunk of material to me. Within minutes a well-groomed woman arrived. She had a packet of papers under her arm. She exuded professionalism with her dark tailored suit, perhaps compliments of the tailor shop."

"Sophia didn't tell you why you were there?" Margaret asked.

Margaret looked as if she were trying to figure me out as much as Sophia.

"No," I said. "Sophia just said that she needed to visit a friend of hers."

John nudged Margaret and said, "There's one born every twenty seconds."

"Cute," I said and continued with my story, "The woman introduced herself as Mrs. Graetal Dobruja, the agency representative. There was no small talk. 'You are interested in Sophia to come to your home in the United States?' she asked in studied English.

121

"I was stunned. I didn't know what to say. The woman went on, 'Your son is how old?' 'Almost six,' I said. The woman cracked a somewhat superior smile and began to translate letters of recommendation on behalf of Sophia. She dropped in words such as: Extraordinary, excellence, crème de la crème, utmost morality. After she was certain that I got the message, she asked me for *cash!*"

"Did you fork over the beans?" Margaret asked, grounded in reality.

"Are you serious?" I said, "I sat there dumbfounded. The woman began to explain that Sophia was a citizen of an Eastern-bloc country. She said that Romania had a relatively liberal emigration policy, but it didn't extend to the au pair tradition. She went on about how the government of President Nicolae Ceausescu now allowed for foreign exchange students to enter the U.S. Sophia could apply for a foreign exchange-student visa. But to do this she needed, *cash*. Two thousand dollars."

"Holy FUBAR!" Margaret said.

"That's Marine for 'fucked up by Army regulations," Chris explained.

"I told the woman that I thought Sophia was wonderful, but I had to first check with my husband. Then I gave Sophia a weak smile. She returned a weak smile. And in that moment, I swear that her gums receded to make them apppear jutting. vampirelike."

"Oh, Liz," John grumbled.

Margaret definitely appeared to be more amused by John's reaction than my recollection.

"You know how vampires must never see their own reflection. I took out my compact mirror and put on some lipstick. Then I passed the compact to Sophia. 'Do you need to freshen up your lipstick?' I asked. "She seemed to recoil."

"Facts," John said, as the waiter gave us each a dessert menu.

"I'm telling you—she pulled away from the compact."

"Lizzy!" John said to Margaret's undiminished laughter.

"We all ordered the Japanese fried ice cream, the house spe-

cial, and then Margaret regaled us with one of her favorite
stories. Perhaps it was the two Sapporas and saki chaser that
inspired her.

"On July 21, 1944, when the Marines took Guam, two gook
kamikazes fled into the jungle . . ."

"Margaret!" John adominished.

"Two Oriental one-way Zero flyers fled into the jungle,"
Margaret corrected. "They didn't want to be captured by
American ground troops. Their names were Hito and Ninagawa. They stayed hidden in the jungle until 1964. Twenty
years."

"Tell them what they ate," Chris said to Margaret. Apparently he had heard the story before.

"Margaret rattled off: "Coconuts, breadfruit, bamboo shoots,
lizards, snails, snakes, seaweed, lobster."

"They didn't know the war was over," Chris stressed. "They
thought the Marines were there to KATN."

"KATN?" I said.

"Kick ass and take names," Chris explained as Margaret went
on with her story.

"In a few weeks their sense of smell became like an animal's.
They could sniff the hair tonic of Americans before they heard
them."

"Sometimes they lived in a cave!" Chris said.

"Fuckin' A," Margaret slipped. "They had only their gook
uniforms on their backs."

"Sarge, tell them how they got a fire going."

"When the sun was shinin'," Sarge began, "they used the
bottom of a bottle as a burning glass. And when it was rainin'
they ripped open a cartridge, mixed some powder, dry leaves
and wood shavings. Then they rubbed a piece of wire along a
tree until it got red hot and shoved it into the tinder. Bingo.
Blaze."

"It's amazing that they didn't get sick and die," I said.

"They found natural remedies," Margaret said. "They'd kill
an animal. Rip open its stomach for the gastric juice. Then
they'd dry it in the sun and use it for a tonic."

"Yeah," Chris said, "and they'd make charcoal from wild boar bones. They'd grind it into a powder and that would cure diarrhea . . . diarrhea . . . when you're driving in your Chevy and you're feeling a little heavy . . ."

"Mr. Unger could have used some of that," Margaret chuckled while Chris practically rolled off his seat in laughter.

"How'd they finally give themselves up?" John asked.

"Photo reconnaissance convinced the Marines that there were hundreds of sanryusha—enemy stragglers—just like Hito and Ninagawa. The Marines staged a 'leaflet raid.' Hito found one of the leaflets saying that the war was over and Japan and the U.S. were friends. Hito thought it was a trick. So he responded by carvin' his name into the side of a tree along a path that was well traveled by American soldiers. A Marine saw the sign and reported it to the Japanese ministry. They contacted Hito's wife. He hadn't seen her for over *ten* years. She wrote Hito a letter that was dropped at the site of the tree where he carved his name. She told him that they had a son and that the war was over. But the letter never reached Hito. Every so often the Marines would drop bundles of Tokyo newspapers into the jungle. Hito thought it could be enemy propaganda. And when he saw a picture of a slope kissin' an American soldier, he was convinced it was. So him and Ninagawa retreated deeper into the jungle."

"Yeah," Chris said, "and they stayed there for eight more years before they were captured by the *Marines.*"

There was no doubt in my mind Chris was headed for the Academy.

"When the Marines choppered Hito and Ninagawa back to Tokyo they thought they were goin' be tossed out over the Pacific. And when they were taken to base hospital and given a medical examination prior to being reunited with their families, the two dip-dunks thought they were gettin' ready to be executed," Margaret said, looking from John to me, as if the United States Marines would be capable of doing something as heartless as that.

"What a story," I said.

"Damn interesting," John said. He signaled the waiter for the check.

As we drove home, Margaret was telling Chris: "A well-executed amphibious assault is as beautiful a military spectacle as one can find in warfare."

CHAPTER 14

TOWARD THE END OF SUMMER, Margaret seemed to come to terms with the fact that she would never have a relationship with her mother. Unlike when she first returned from Pensacola, Margaret was now full of enthusiasm and ideas. Margaret and Chris were always off on some adventure, and when they were hanging around the house they were planning mock invasions of one sort or another. Neither John nor I mentioned the Pensacola incident. We figured that if she wanted to talk about it she could bring it up. She never did. I noticed, however, that above her bed she pinned the following quote: "I have always believed that God never gives a cross to bear larger than we can carry. No matter what, he wants us to be happy, not sad. Birds sing after a storm. Why shouldn't we?—Rose Kennedy."

The quotation hung next to her poster of the U.S.S *Intrepid*. Chris had the same poster. They were souvenirs of the day Margaret took Chris to the Air & Sea Museum in New York.

On the afternoon that Margaret and Chris were off touring Sikorsky Helicopter, I went into town to do some shopping. As I passed our local parfumerie, I saw Janet at the counter. I went in expecting to hear almost anything. I was not disappointed.

"How's this smell?" she asked, squirting me with Obsession for Men.

"Too spicy," I said, imagining Janet spritzing Danny—all over.

"How 'bout the Halston?" she asked, drenching my other arm.

"Better," I said.

"I'll take the Halston," Janet said. She pulled out a lace G-string and asked the girl behind the counter, "What goes with this?"

"Michael Bolton," the clerk said, annoyed that Janet had interrupted her from blending her eyeshadow.

"Try this Indian Earth," I said.

Janet sampled the blush, "Howie and I are dating."

"What?"

"Two weeks ago he had matinee tickets to *Les Misérables* and so I went."

I thought: A matinee ticket to *Les Misérables* is all it takes. What would an evening performance of *Cats* do?

"You're getting back together?"

"We have a *sixteen*-year history."

"Iwo Jima fell after 500 years," I said, wondering if my history was even in the ball park.

"It's mainly for the kids. And my mother. His mother . . ."

"And the dog," I said.

"Poor Max," Janet said, smoothing the blush. "In people-years he's one hundred and five."

"Danny's out of the picture then?"

Janet plunked down her Visa, "I can't keep seeing Danny if there's a chance Howie and I can make it."

"How's Danny taking all of this?"

"Devastated," Janet said. "But he's going to try to make it with his wife."

"Wife?"

"He claimed that they hadn't slept together in years." Janet said. "A dead relationship. I know I shouldn't have believed him. But I did."

I recalled a bumper sticker I read off a Volvo: YOU CAN TELL

Elizabeth Fuller

A MAN IS LYING IF HE MOVES HIS LIPS. I didn't need to share this with Janet. I think it was on her car.

"How you going to get over him?" I asked. I, too, sampled the Indian Earth.

"According to my chart, by November Pluto is going to square my house of romance."

Astrology made a big comeback in Westport when the Crystal Diva opened up and offered free charts when you bought two pairs of earrings.

"We're working on the sex," Janet whispered. She had a faint smile.

That was up for grabs.

"After he found out about Danny and me he couldn't do it with Helga anymore. She could yodel her brains out and it remained as limp as string cheese."

"Are you saying Helga confessed?"

"Didn't Margaret tell you?"

"No."

"Helga told me that she told Margaret," Janet said.

"Margaret never gossips," I said.

"Then she didn't tell you what she did to Howard?"

"Margaret did something to Howard?"

"Let's get an espresso at the Pasta Patio," Janet said. "You *have* to hear this one."

"The day after I threw Howie out," Janet said, grabbing a corner table next to the rack of imported olive oil, "Margaret and Darlene came by looking for Helga. They were going to the Tin Whistle. I told them that Helga was staying with Howie at his office. They could find her there. The girls showed up unexpectedly, surprising the two. They heard screaming. Margaret kicked in the door and found Helga tied upside down in the chair, yodeling with a mouth full of . . ."

"Oh, my God," I said, thinking, shades of the Castro Convertible.

"Margaret untied Helga, made sure she was okay. Then she said to Howie . . ."

128

"Let me guess," I interrupted, "She said, 'Pussywimp, hit the deck and give me fifty!'"
Janet looked startled. "How'd you know?"
"I just know Margaret," I said.

About two months after Margaret's fateful trip to Pensacola, her father sent a letter with news that brightened all of our lives.

"Dear Daughter:
Since our last correspondence, I have decided to make a major change in my life. Perhaps this change was triggered by the many things you wrote. I take comfort in that you have found a compassionate family. I realize your duty is to look after their youngster. But I'm grateful that they are looking after my daughter, especially at this time. I was never optimistic about your quest to find your mother. I was hoping to be proved wrong.
Daughter, I have decided to get married to Mary Ellen, the head nurse at base hospital. As you will recall, she was at my side morning, noon and night. I think the first day the doctor let me walk, you were holding me up on one side and Mary Ellen the other as I wobbled down the corridor.
Mary Ellen will be retiring in just another year—about six months after my retirement. I thought that since she is from California, we could retire out there, buy a small place with a guest room for you to come and visit as often as you can. Mary Ellen never had a daughter. She has four sons.
After reading your last letter many times over, I've decided not to drag my feet on this decision. Thank you for the beautiful quote by Rose Kennedy. I have it on my bedside table.
Mary Ellen and I have set a November 30th wedding date— provided Mr. and Mrs. Fuller will give you the time off. My only regret is that I didn't find Mary Ellen years earlier so you could have benefitted from this fine woman. Like my childlren, her sons were all in the military. Mary Ellen will be writing to you

in the next few days. She hopes you will agree to be her maid of honor.

I wish you fair weather and following winds.

Love,
Dad

P.S. Please tell Mr. Fuller that I'm thoroughly engrossed in his new book: *The Day We Bombed Utah*. It's hard to believe that our government could be responsible for such negligence. On a lighter note, Mary Ellen and I are still roaring over Mrs. Fuller almost bringing a vampire home to take care of her youngster. Sounds like there's never a dull moment with your family.

Margaret's spirits soared as she prepared for her father's upcoming wedding.

CHAPTER 15

MARGARET AND I spent the entire month of September in search of the perfect dress for the wedding. After hitting every store between Connecticut and New York, Margaret chose an emerald green off-the-shoulder from a boutique right in town.

"Dearie," the saleslady said, "that dress was begging for hazel eyes and red hair."

My input was to convince Margaret that it needed to be shortened to just above the knee to show off her great legs.

"You'll get the full effect of how fabulous you're going to look when you take off your glasses and style your hair," the saleslady said as she boxed the gown.

Our next stop was LensCrafters for Margaret's first pair of contact lenses. Then we dropped in on Mr. Anthony.

"Where on *earth* did you get your last haircut? The Marines?" he had one eye in the mirror and the other on Margaret's camouflage T-shirt . . .

When he swept away to get his appointment book, Margaret commented: "Lead weights in his cowboy boots should keep him on the deck."

"I can fit you in next Wednesday," Mr. Anthony said, preoccupied with a spot on his Henry Lehr silk shirt.

"Can't make it," Margaret said.

Mr. Anthony's full attention turned to Margaret's blatant lack of respect for his time and talent.

That night I realized that Margaret had become a beauty. John didn't
even recognize her. "Margaret," he finally said, "you keep dressing
like that and we're going to lose the best nanny we ever had."

"Then you'll have to wait until Saturday at nine," he slapped his book closed, and straightened the cowboy hat that he picked up in Taos.

"How much?" Margaret asked.

Mr. Anthony's fine senses were being assaulted left and right.

"Seventy-five for the first cut," he said.

"How come so cheap?" Margaret asked.

"Margaret," I said, "he means seventy-five dollars. But it's my treat."

It took several moments for Margaret to process the price. "Tony cuts it for nine at the barber shop," Margaret said. "When Nick's there I get a Marine discount."

Mr. Anthony adjusted the Navaho clip on his pony tail, and said to me: "Is she serious?"

"Twelve dollars," Margaret said.

"This isn't a Baghdad spice bazaar," Mr. Anthony snapped.

"This isn't Tombstone, Arizona either," Margaret said, giving his Wyatt Earp outfit a once-over.

I turned to Mr. Anthony and said, "We'll give you a call."

Mr. Anthony didn't dignify us with a response. He simply breezed off, calling to the receptionist: "Chloe, Chloe. I'm too *exhausted* for my two o'clock. She'll have to wait. You can find me in the color room."

The evening Margaret put it all together, I realized that she was damned beautiful. When we called John down from his office to see the final results, he didn't recognize her.

"You really don't know who that is?" I asked John. Christopher was in the corner covering his mouth.

John studied the slim girl standing only ten feet away and apologized, "I'm afraid I don't know this very pretty girl."

"Give him a clue, Sarge," Chris said, blowing her cover.

"Margaret?" John said, not believing his eyes.

"Aye, aye, sir."

"Margaret," John said, "you keep dressing like that and we're going to lose the best nanny we ever had."

Margaret smiled shyly. I'm sure she had no idea how attractive she was. This brought up another point. I had never really thought about Margaret being romantically involved. But on one of our recent shopping excursions, Margaret told me about a boyfriend she had just before she was riffed—budget cutback. He was a helicopter pilot. They were going to get married. But then he met a townie and all that changed. That's when Margaret packed up the Mustang and headed north.

I always wondered what propelled her to pack up and leave. I should have known it was a guy. It's always a guy.

The day Margaret told me this, I asked, "Have you gotten over him?"

Talking about feelings did not come easily to her. Margaret showed me a photo of him. He was in the cockpit of his helicopter.

"Nice looking," I said.

Margaret was noncommital.

"Whatever happened to him?"

"He married the townie. They split six months later."

"Have you talked to him since?" I asked, hoping I wasn't overstepping my bounds.

Margaret nodded.

I didn't want to push it so I let it drop. But she surprisingly didn't let it drop.

"When I was in Pensacola I called Rob . . ."

"His name is Rob?"

"Yep," Margaret said. "He told me he made a big mistake. Him and the townie had nothin' in common. She pushed papers in an insurance office. She became hysterical when he was sent to the Gulf. He came back to find her shacked up with her old boyfriend—a mechanic at the Mobil station."

"Would you go back with him?"

"What for?" Margaret asked.

"Because you seem to care," I said.

"I was dumped once," she said.

"It hurts."

"Yes, ma'am."

"You know, Margaret, if I had a nickel for every time I was dumped . . ."

"You've been dumped a lot?" Margaret asked.

"Fuckin' A," I said.

Margaret snickered.

"But then I met John. He changed my life. I told you how I met him on a flight."

"I love it when you said, 'Excuse me, sir, are you the writer?' And he said: 'You the stewardess?'"

"You gotta kiss a lot of frogs, Margaret."

"Ma'am," Margaret said, suddenly dead serious, "how'd you know you loved John?"

"I was totally taken with him," I said. "Maybe it was because he was so accomplished. Then again, maybe it was because he saw things in me that I didn't even know existed. He was the *first* person to tell me that I had talent. Oh, I don't know, Margaret. There's not one reason that I fell for him. Chemistry. We clicked. Everybody said that our marriage was doomed. Our age difference. It turned out that the only thing that was doomed was the prediction."

"Maybe I'll send Rob a picture of Cruit and me at Sikorsky," Margaret said.

"Hey, that's a good idea."

It was about a week after we had that conversation that Margaret knocked on my office door. "Ma'am," she said, "you have a minute?"

Margaret never interrupted us during our writing hours. Something must have been up.

"You win the lottery?" I asked. Every straight white tooth in Margaret's mouth was on display.

"I just got a letter," she said.

At first I thought it was from her father. Margaret always read every letter he wrote before it went into her scrap book.

"I'm ready to hear," I said.

But Margaret wasn't ready to read it. "It's from *Rob*," she said.

"Chopper Rob?"

"Yes, ma'am. He thanked me for the picture."

"So you sent him the photo of you and Chris at Sikorsky?"

"We were standin' in front of a Jolly Green Giant," Margaret said.

"A what?"

"A 53–E," Margaret said.

"A chopper?"

"Yes, ma'am."

"Did he say anything else?" I asked.

"He said that the government's cuttin' back on the Super-stallion."

"That's all he said?"

"No, ma'am. He wanted to know if we got a look at the fiberglass body. Kevlar. When a bullet goes in the kevlar it comes out the same diameter. Miracle material. It doesn't spread."

"Is that it?" I said.

"No, ma'am. He wanted to know if we got a look at the rotor heads."

"I see," I said, thinking that this was a match made in heaven. How could Chopper Rob have possibly lasted with the townie shuffling fire, theft and auto applications?

Margaret scanned the letter, "On his last search and destroy mission, heavy ground fire damaged the landin' gear. He damn near had to do a belly landing out of LZ."

"LZ?"

"Landing zone."

"Sounds like a real newsy letter," I said.

"He's gonna write again when he gets back from a mine-sweep maneuver in the ocean."

"I can see why you're beaming," I said.

The following day Chris and Margaret went back up to Sikorsky to check out the rotor heads. Margaret's Olympus was loaded. She hoped that they'd be allowed to take pictures. When they left the house, Margaret was wearing the new contact lenses. Her camouflage trousers were neatly bloused inside spit-shined boots. Chris and Margaret were wearing matching U.S.S. *Intrepid* T-shirts. Margaret's new hairstyle by Tina at Hair

Works, looked fresh and bouncy—with tip it came to $16.95. "They don't give Marine discounts," Margaret said, "but they threw in the conditioner."

Eat your heart out, Wyatt Earp.

As I watched the two hop into the Mustang, I thought that if Margaret were on the streets of New York she could easily pass for a model in funky clothes on the way to a shoot. Wait until Rob sees what he gave up.

I called out to the car, "Chris, take a lot of pictures of Margaret!"

"Yes, ma'am," he called back.

I went into the house to find John in bed.

"You okay?" I asked. John never slept in the middle of the day. Sometimes he'd have a catnap in his reclining office chair. But he *never* went to bed.

"Just tired," he said.

I didn't like his coloring. "You don't look good," I said, feeling his forehead. He was sweaty.

"I'll be okay," he said. "I guess I have a slight pain."

"A pain!"

"It'll go away," he said.

"Where is it?"

"Here," he said, pointing to the center of his chest.

"I'm calling Dr. Steinberg," I said.

"It's going away now," he said, getting up.

"Don't get up," I said.

"Lizzy it's gone."

"Are you *sure*?"

"Positive."

"But don't get up just yet," I said. "Rest for a while."

"I'm fine," he insisted. "I've got to get chapter ten in the mail."

"Let me call Dr. Steinberg."

"Where's Chris?" John asked, moments before he collapsed back onto the bed.

CHAPTER 16

I FOLLOWED THE AMBULANCE to the hospital. By the time I parked the car, John was in the emergency room. I was told to go to the waiting room. The moment they assessed the situation the nurse would come for me.

The television was blaring. Two elderly ladies next to me were watching a soap opera. During the commercial they were discussing the characters' TV lives as if they mattered. What about the four trillion dollar deficit? Working class families slipping into poverty? What about *my* husband?

I was getting ready to ask if they wouldn't mind turning the volume down when Dr. Steinberg appeared.

"Liz," he said, grinning, "John's telling the nurse a bunch of bad jokes. You'd better get in there fast."

I burst into tears. "John's okay?" I asked.

"We know one thing for sure: He didn't have a heart attack."

"What caused the pain?"

"We need to run tests," he said, stroking one of the eight pens in his pocket.

"Maybe it was just heartburn?" I said to myself.

As we headed toward the emergency room, I suddenly recalled the last time I had walked along the sterile corridor. It was during Wendy's stint with us.

She was the nanny who displayed palpable signs of amnesia on rainy days or during high humidity. Anyway, it was during a stationary front of lousy weather that Wendy became pregnant. When the dry, sunny weather finally arrived, Wendy had *no* recollection of getting herself in a family way. To make matters worse, she had absolutely *no* recall of the fellow who took advantage of her in the sticky, drizzling month of June.

Since Wendy didn't know she was pregnant, she went waterskiing on Long Island Sound. It was a beautiful clear day. John and I felt comfortable about her going off with a few of her friends in our car. Earlier that morning we had turned on Willard Scott and learned that high pressure from the Midwest would bring clear sunny skies for the next twenty-four to forty-eight hours.

Wendy left the house complaining that she had slight cramps. She chalked it up to getting her period, grabbed the car keys and left the house singing. Wendy never sang in the rain. During precipitation she couldn't remember lyrics.

At around midnight, Wendy came to our bedroom, doubled over with cramps. John and I packed her into the car. I drove her to the hospital where she miscarried. She had been six weeks pregnant.

"I'm not pregnant!" Wendy said indignantly to the young, foreign intern.

"You are not pregnant now," he said in a singsong Indian accent.

"Like you have to have s-e-x to get pregnant," Wendy spit.

"In my country that is true," said this Gandhi clone.

"Aha mah Gawd, I am so grossed out." said this East Coast Valley Girl. "I really need to see like a doctor."

"I am a medical doctor. . ."

God, every Indian I'd ever met was a "medical doctor." Weren't there any plumbers or insurance adjusters out of New Delhi?

"What is wrong with that young woman?" the doctor asked when we were alone.

"Oh," I said, off the record, "Wendy is absolutely great in a dry climate. But about six weeks ago . . . you know the lousy June we had. . ."

139

He cut me off as only "medical docctors" can. "I do not understand your point."

I told him all about the effect the weather had on Wendy, and of course, I explained that is was because of the metal plate in her head. "It must be rusty," I said to his wide-eyed glare.

"That is pure poppycock," he said. His beeper went off and he disappeared.

That all seemed like light-years away. Now, as Dr. Steinberg and I neared one of the antiseptic cubbies in the emergency room, I heard John's raspy voice. For a moment I thought I spotted the Indian doctor. I quickly looked the other way.

John was sitting up doing just what Dr. Steinberg said, telling jokes to the nurse who had him hooked up to a cardiac monitor.

"*Here's* my wife!" John said.

He was always so proud of me. I would have to remember to tell Margaret that that was another reason why I fell for him. He thought I was the most beautiful woman he had ever seen.

"You look like you're ready to take off," I said, planting a quick kiss on the top of his head. I tried to avoid looking at all the wires that ran from his extremities to the machine. I kept telling myself that he would be okay, but suddenly something just didn't feel right.

"They want to keep me overnight," John said. "What did we have planned with Chris?"

"Just a picnic at the beach," I said. "We'll do it tomorrow night."

"Good idea," John said. In that instant, something I read in his eyes told me that on some level he, too, knew that something was seriously wrong.

The following week, my worst fears were realized.

"Liz," Dr. Steinberg said over the phone, "I have some bad news for you."

It was indeed bad news. John had lung cancer. He was given six months to live. He died in two.

NANNIES

The Friday before he died, John went back into the hospital for the last time. Chris and I were with John the evening he died. He left us at 5:40 P.M. I'll never forget that time. Because at five o'clock, after drifting in and out of consciousness all day, he opened his eyes, searched the room for Christopher, and motioned for the nurse to take off his oxygen mask.

"Come here, Scooter," he said, his voice faint but audible.

Scooter was a long-forgotten nickname John had given Chris as a toddler.

Chris, frightened but brave, went to his dad's bedside. Then with an energy that came from some divine source, John began to sing a song he sang the first time he held Christopher. It was Cole Porter's "You're the Top." Over the years, it went on to become "their" song.

"You're the top!" John sang through parched lips. "You're the Colosseum. You're the top! You're the Louvre Museum. . . You're the smile on the Mona Lisa. . ."

Chris gently stroked his father's bruised and thin arm as he waited to sing his favorite part.

John nodded to Chris, cuing him.

"You're Mickey Mouse!" Chris belted out just as he had in better days.

The next time we heard that song was at John's memorial service. It was a musical service. With John's two sons, Jeff and Judd, playing his favorite music: Cole Porter, Sam Cooke and jazz. No rock 'n' roll.

CHAPTER 17

THE FIRST SIX MONTHS after John's death have all become a blur. Margaret canceled her trip to Okinawa. She said that there was *no* way she was going to leave her family in time of mourning to dance at a wedding. If Margaret was the celestial cement who kept our lives glued together, Chris was the divine spark who had a philosophy that seemed so far beyond his years.

"Mom," he said, "you're making Dad sad because you stopped writing."

"Why do you say that Chris?"

"Because before he ever even played ball with me, he wanted to read what you wrote. That made him laugh real loud. We can't see Dad but he's here. And it's making him sad that you're not working anymore. And it's making me sad because Dad died singing and you cry all day."

I cried all that night, and the next morning, I went to my office and picked up where I left off six months earlier. For the next half-year I buried myself in my work, and *only* my work. And then Margaret said something that would shock me back into the world of the living.

"Ma'am," she said, "Cruit lost his father a year ago this month. And he lost his mother at the same time."

I became defensive. "For God's sake Margaret, I'm here all day!"

"Ma'am, you work *all* day. And on weekends. You even worked on Thanksgiving morning. Remember we planned it to be a family day? Cruit and I ended up doin' the turkey by ourselves."

NANNIES

"Margaret!" I snapped. "somebody has to pay these bills!"

"And somebody has to realize that John Fuller is *not* going to walk back into this house. But Christopher Fuller is in the kitchen right *now* chowin' down without his mother!"

Margaret showed me a drawing Chris had brought home from school. It depicted a house. It was our house. There were four windows. Two had curtains. Inside the other two windows Chris had drawn Margaret and himself.

"Ma'am, you're not in Cruit's picture."

I stared at the drawing. I'm not a psychologist, but common sense told me that Margaret was right. I had dropped out of my son's life. I had dropped out of life.

Later that day I went to Margaret's room.

"Margaret," I said, reading Rose Kennedy's quote on her wall, "Birds sing after a storm, why shouldn't we?"

A smile broke across Margaret's face. She put down her book: *Victory in the Pacific* and said, "Cruit and I are plannin' 'Operation Iceberg,' ma'am. You want to join us?"

"I was thinking more in terms of a manuever in the Pacific," I said.

Margaret looked quizzical.

"Margaret," I said, "let's go to California for Christmas. You remember me talking about my friend Silvie?"

"The one who used to live down the road?"

"That's right. She's invited us for Christmas. We'll have a ball. We'll go absolutely everywhere. No stone unturned. We'll go to Disneyland. You've never been there . . ."

"Yes! Yes! Yes!" Chris said bursting into Margaret's room just in time to hear the news. "We're going to Auntie Sylvie's!"

This was double good news for Margaret. Rob was stationed at Camp Pendleton.

"I want you to write Rob and tell him we're coming out December sixteenth," I said.

Margaret's eyes twinkled like Christmas tree ornaments.

"Yes, ma'am," she said.

"And we both need some new clothes," I said.

"I'm not going shopping!" Chris said.

"Margaret, it looks like just you and I will be going on a mall manuever," I said, ready to join the world of the living.

The evening before we left for California, Janet insisted on having us over for dinner.

"Bring the kids," Janet said, "Darlene and Margaret can take them to the movies and McDonald's, and we'll have a quiet dinner around the fire."

The quiet dinner around the fire consisted of Howard, Janet and Leonard, a recently divorced divorce lawyer who was under some impression that he was Marvin Mitchelson and I was Lee Marvin's ex waiting to happen.

"Nice to meet you," I said, eyeballing the loafers and no socks. I always wanted to ask if their feet stuck? Did it wreck the shoe? Did they use foot powder? My eyes went from his loafers to his hair. He had one of those contrived hairdos to cover the bald parts. It swirled and dipped and dipped and swirled. John was bald and could have cared less. All right, I said to myself, just because Leonard had a golf course on his head was no reason to make value judgments.

"Leonard handles the biggest divorce cases in Fairfield County," Howard said, checking out Margaret's butt as she left the house with Darlene and the kids.

"I'm never getting married again," Leonard said, comparing my breasts to Janet's.

"So, I'll have to take back the gown?" I was tempted to say.

Over drinks he laid a bomb, "I can't deal with other people's kids."

"So, I'll kill the kid," I was a breath away from saying.

"Anybody seen any good movies?" Janet asked, placing a tray of dim sum on top of the Andy Warhol coffee-table book.

"Margaret and I just rented *Shirley Valentine*," I said. "It was terrific."

"I'm dying to see it," Janet said.

"I plopped down five bucks to watch a fat lady kvetch," Howard said charging for the dim sum.

"And I wasted an evening watching dim sum squirt out of

some guy's mouth when I could be home packing," I wanted to say.

"How old's your son?" Howard asked, mentally calculating my age. His eyes were glued to my limbs. If he'd had a hatchet he could've counted the rings.

"I had him when I was sixty-two," I thought about saying.

"Nine," I said.

"Leonard's a barracuda," said Howard the sperm whale.

I got up and went to the kitchen to help Janet.

"What do you think?" Janet said over the sizzling wok.

"A little more of that Bangkok peanut sauce," I said.

"No," Janet said. "I mean Leonard."

Truth or consequences? "Nice guy, but not for me." I said.

Janet reached for the Chinese cooking wine and said, "I didn't think you'd like him."

"Janet, why did you do this to me?"

"It was Howie's idea. He thought you should start meeting people."

I thought: If anybody should know about meeting people it was Howie.

"But *Leonard?*" I said.

"Howie had me convinced that he changed after his divorce. He joined some men's movement and went on a wilderness journey to get in touch with his essence. I really don't know all the details," Janet apologized.

Over dessert I heard all the details.

"We gathered in clans to experience 'self,'" Leonard told us. "For a week, eight men ran around naked, two lawyers, a doctor, a dentist, accountant . . ."

The imagery was killing me.

"During daylight we'd go 'tracking.' Following our instincts. Hunting prey. Eating wild berries. Roots. Killing a buffalo . . ."

Like this Davy Crockett really nailed a buffalo.

". . . at sunset, we'd break off into small groups and chant to the gods, getting in touch with our primitive masculine side . . ."

As Bette Davis would say: I think I'm going to vaaaaahmit!

"There were days when I just rolled in the grass, eating and sniffing the earth. Talking to rocks. The last day I hugged a hundred-and-fifty-year-old oak from dawn to dusk . . ."

And he was so concerned over my age?

Leonard gave Margaret and me a lot to chat about on the six-hour flight to L.A.

"Margaret," I said, "I don't want to get involved in the dating scene. I'll never find anyone I can relate to the way I did to John."

Margaret flopped her book, *Pacific War Diary*, onto the tray table, "Ma'am, the C.O. is goin' be a hard act to follow."

"You got that one right," I said, thinking about all the times John and I had driven by the Unitarian Church where the singles meet each week, and how smug we were that we had each other. We didn't have to suffer hearing: "So what's your sign? or "Do you rent or own?" or "Have you been tested?"

Margaret unwrapped a wedge of cheese and said as only Margaret could say: "Ma'am you sure did hit two dip-dunks."

Leonard was my *second* encounter after John's death. Gil was my first. After our initial date, he sent a dozen long-stemmed red roses with a note: "Close your eyes and think of me and soon I will be there to brighten up even your darkest nights."

Reading the florist card, I thought: Does he have to pay royalty to Roberta Flack?

On the next date, he gave me a video of Charlie Chaplin. Not a bad thought. How was he supposed to know I didn't like Chaplin? He insisted that we watch it before we left for the movies, although he had seen it over fifty times. Five minutes into the movie, Chris nestled between us with his new hand buzzer. Gil ordered Chris out of the room: "Out of here with that, kid!" Then this highly sensitive man used half a box of Kleenex during the scene where Chaplin is cruelly rejected by a girl working in a flower shop.

After the silent flick, Chris dropped the old fly in the ice into Gil's drink, "Knock it off, kid!"

I am Woman, hear me roar!

"Mom," Chris said as we watched Gil pull his Lexus out of

the driveway, "I'm glad you changed your mind about going to the movies with him. He cries too loud."

Now, as I looked out the window at the Grand Canyon below, that all seemed even more ridiculous. I wanted more from life than the Gils and the Leonards. With each passing month since John's death, I began to actually believe that I was a total person in my own right. I didn't need a man just because as my mother said: "Liz, it would be so nice if you could find someone for you and Chris. A boy needs a father." Maybe she was right, but I couldn't go out and just look for one. Besides, I believed enough in the spiritual world that when the time was right, someone would be there for us. And if there wasn't, I could live a complete life by myself. I didn't need a man to validate my self-worth, and for that I felt free—sometimes bordering on smug. Chris seemed adjusted. Of course he missed his dad. They were like two peas in a pod. But I felt as if I were doing an okay job as both mother and father. I took Chris to Cub Scout meetings, helped him make the soapbox cars, camped out, pitched balls, scolded him in a deep voice when he got out of hand. I had to laugh thinking about how only days after John's death, I went to the hardware store in town and bought a glue gun, an ax and a wheelbarrow, as if that would beef up my testosterone level.

"Margaret," I said, looking down at the Grand Canyon. "let's go on an adventure."

Margaret adjusted a pillow under Chris's head, "We *are* goin' on an adventure, ma'am."

"I mean a *real* adventure!" I said. "Just look at the way the sun and shadow reveal those mesas. I want to show Chris the world. I want to show him Australia. The Outback. All he knows is suburbia," I said, clumsily spilling coffee onto my new Liz Claiborne shirt.

I could see in Margaret's eyes that she didn't share my enthusiasm. I tempered my statement. "But let's first see how this trip goes."

I recalled the letter Rob had written Margaret two days earlier. He asked if she would be able to stay with him for at least part of the vacation. He'd take a leave. They'd take the Jeep along the coast. Stop at the officer's club in Monterey. Visit former shore installations. Hike. Swim. He signed off: Love, Rob.

Margaret hesitated to tell me all of this. "Ma'am," she said, showing me his letter, "mind if I spend some time with Rob?"

"Holy Fubar!" I said, throwing my arms around her, "you're going to have the time of your life!"

"You sure it's okay?"

"It's not okay," I said. "It's fantastic. But we didn't get you a dress."

"I've got that green wedding dress I never wore."

"Way too dressy for an officer's club," I said.

That afternoon Margaret and I went back to the mall. I felt like a mother helping her daughter buy her honeymoon outfit. And if I want to be totally honest, I did feel a tiny twinge of jealousy. I was losing Margaret to Rob. What was it my mother always said, "Give them roots and wings."

"Excuse me, ma'am," Margaret said to the flight attendant, "can you tell me the maximum gross weight and maximum range on this Douglas DC–10?"

The flight attendant said she'd find out. A few moments later the captain announced that the gross weight was 580,000 pounds and the range was 7,475 miles. Margaret wrote it in her diary.

It was amazing that Margaret and I hit it off so well. I didn't have a clue how an airplane stayed in the air, nor did I care.

Rob was as attractive as his photos. He was tall with thick sandy hair that wasn't as close-cropped as I had imagined. But his wide smile was his best feature just as Margaret had said.

"Hi, big guy," he said to Chris.

Chris smiled shyly. I couldn't help but wonder if he felt a little jealous.

"Let's see if this fits," Rob said, plunking a U.S. Marine cap onto Chris's head.

"Wow, thanks!" Chris said, instantly bonding.

"Can you spend some time with me, too?" Chris asked.

"Margaret and I have some place special we're takin' you."

"Where?" Chris asked, sandwiched between Margaret and Rob.

"If we told you, you wouldn't be surprised," Rob said, admiring Margaret.

"You look terrific," he said to her. Then he whispered something and she giggled. I think it was the first time I had ever heard Margaret giggle.

As with Margaret, Rob had a story. Rob's father was a Marine physician. He was killed in Vietnam while loading wounded onto a helicopter during the battle at Khe San. Rob was only nine. Chris's age. A year after he was killed, Rob's mother married an enlisted man who beat her as part of a day's routine. At sixteen, Rob came home from school to find his mother on the floor, bruised and bleeding. When his stepfather stumbled in from the local bar, Rob evened the score. That same night, Rob packed up his mother and two sisters and drove to his grandmother's house in North Carolina.

"Guess what, Rob?" Chris said as we walked toward Baggage Claim, "Me and Sarge saw the HH–53H at Sikorsky."

"What's an HH–53H, champ?" Rob challenged his new little buddy.

"It's a Sea Stallion chopper loaded for Spec War operations," Chris said with no uncertainty.

"Slap me five!" Rob said.

Margaret beamed.

The ten days flew by—literally. The day before we left, Rob took Margaret, Chris and me up in his friend's Piper Cherokee, a single-engine four-seater, and gave us a bird's-eye view of Camp Pendleton, and the Gulf of Santa Catalina.

Rob was in the left-hand seat, Chris was in the copilot's seat and Margaret and I were in the back. After pointing out the expansive Marine base, Rob headed out over the water. There wasn't a cloud in the sky. The sun glistened off the water. Clusters of billowing sailboats drifted below. I had a sense of freedom and inner calm. Life was good. It was especially good for Margaret. She had spent six of the ten days with Rob. Just watching the two together was life-affirming. It made me question if maybe there was somebody out there for me? And for Chris?

Although Chris was doing fine coping with the loss of his father, I could see by the way he embraced Rob that he missed the male force in his life. I had to smile thinking of the holiday party at school. Chris had purposely seated me next to the divorced father of one of his classmates, and then encouraged conversation between us: "Mom, tell Mr. Lundstrom about the leak we have in our steering wheel column."

By the time we sang: "Deck the Halls," I learned that Sven owned the Saab dealership in town, his former wife was recovering at the Betty Ford Clinic, and Nanny Meg had helped herself to an unregistered Saab and clipped a parked Isuzu Trooper going eighty miles an hour. Between his thick accent and wild hand gestures, I felt as if I were talking to the Swedish chef on "The Muppet Show."

I was jolted out of this reverie when I heard Rob say to Chris: "You wanna fly this bird, Cruit?"

"Is it okay, Mom?" Chris said, shrieking with delight.

"Just hold her steady," Rob said, as Chris grabbed the control yoke.

"Am I doin' good?" Chris asked, turning to look at Margaret.

"Keep your eyes forward, Cruit," Margaret said.

"But I can't see anything," Chris said.

"That's okay," Rob said, "just do what I tell you."

I fought my gut instinct and sat mutely behind my nine-year-old Lindbergh who was flying the plane yet wasn't tall enough to see over the control panel.

"I want you to pull her up slow and easy," Rob said.

Perhaps it was my imagination but the sailboats seemed much more defined than when Rob had the controls.

"Sarge, I'm comin' in for a kikusui attack!" Chris whooped, jerking his head toward Margaret and me. His little eyes were glazed with euphoria.

"Keep your eyes on the instrument panel!" Margaret commanded. Then she joined in the fantasy, "Vertical dive for the Birmingham!"

NANNIES

"Kamikaze!" Chris screeched, making a strident sound effect, simulating an explosion.

"You divebombed the minesweeper!" Rob played along.

"Zeke makin' shallow dive," Chris called, as he tipped the plane perilously close to the white caps.

The inner calm had left me. I didn't want to be a stick in the mud so I kept quiet and wondered how many flight minutes Rob was going to allow Chris to log. I started to feel a little queasy.

"Keep her steady," Rob instructed.

"Rob," I said, "is it okay that he can't see where he's going?"

"He's doin' real good," Rob said so casually that I actually believed him. For a moment my queasiness went away.

"Keep an eye out for more minesweepers," Rob told Chris. Then he turned to Margaret, and began making small talk, "So where should we all chow down tonight?"

I was unnerved. My kamikaze son was the only one keeping an eye on the candy store.

After what seemed like an eternity, Margaret said, "Rob and I are takin' you and Cruit to El Cantino for the best enchiladas."

Oh, God, enchiladas. I was ready to toss my cookies.

"Yummy!" Chris said, dipping the left wing, "I love Mexican."

Were there training wheels for airplanes? Finally Rob checked on Chris. "You're doin' real good, big guy. Just keep holdin' her steady."

Then he once again turned to the object of his affection. "Looks like a regatta down there," Rob said, distracted by the closeness of Margaret. They were looking out the side window, estimating knots while I searched the sky for oncoming air traffic.

I saw Chris's hand inch toward a red control knob located in the middle of the panel. It was labeled, "mixture."

"Chris, what are you doing?" I asked as the engine sputtered and came to a complete halt.

"Oh, shit!" Rob said, snapping to attention.

A pilot once told me that those two words: "Oh, shit" were the last words spoken by pilots on the black box.

151

In my moments of terror, I had a ridiculous thought: Chris's third-grade photo on the front page of the New York *Times* as the pilot who sent us all plummeting into a watery grave.

Rob jammed the red knob forward and the engine fired up again. "Okay, Cruit, I'm going to take over the controls. Good job."

Chris lifted himself. "Wow," he said, "now I can see where we're going."

I learned a lot about Rob that day. I learned that he wanted to build a log cabin in Northern California beside a waterfall, construct a windmill, take a design course so that he could put down on paper a futuristic helicopter. And eventually he wanted to marry someone with whom he saw eye to eye.

"Maybe I'll luck out and have a son as bright as Cruit," Rob said, throwing Chris over his shoulder like a sack of potatoes as we walked through the parking lot to El Cantino.

Margaret giggled.

We arrived home New Year's Eve day. Margaret had plans that night with Darlene and Helga. Helga was now working at the Pasta Patio and sharing a studio apartment at the beach with twins from Wisconsin and a hard-body from San Antonio. All were waiting to be placed with the Hollenbeck Nanny Agency. Mrs. Hollenbeck paid the rent.

From time to time Howard would stop by the Pasta Patio for lunch. But as far as Helga was concerned: *NO MORE MERCY YODELING!*

Chris and I welcomed in the New Year with a liter of Coke and buttered popcorn, and then as we sat cross-legged around the blazing fire we made our New Year's resolutions. I wrote in my journal: I will begin laying the groundwork for us to go live in Australia. I hope that next New Year's Eve, Chris, Margaret and I will be in the sweltering heat, squating in red clay, listening to aboriginal folk tales. I had a fleeting thought that I'd have to get an adaptor for my hairblower.

Chris didn't write anything down, but when I asked him

what his resolution was he said: "Quit school and go live in Australia."

"Hey, how'd you know I wrote about Australia?" I said, showing Chris my journal.

"Mom, that's all you talk about."

"I do?"

"Like only every day, Mom."

"You'll have to go to school, Chris."

"Sarge said I wouldn't have to. I could just take a lot of school books and explore the former dumping ground for criminals!"

Margaret was very hard on other countries. The sun rose and set on the United States—and only the United States.

"Well, I'll have to talk to Sarge about all of this," I said.

"Mom," Chris asked, "how far's Australia from Camp Pendleton?"

"It's far, but not as far as it is from here," I told him. "Margaret will still be able to see Rob. Qantas is always running special fares out of L.A."

Chris had a thousand-mile-stare.

"It's not going to be forever," I said. "Remember Dad used to tell you all those bedtime stories of how before you were born we used to go to remote parts of the world and live for six, nine months, and all the crazy things that happened to us? You couldn't hear enough of those stories."

Chris's face brightened. "Like the holy man in the Himalayas who gave you those little brown pills that were made from his pee and his . . ."

"You got it!" I said.

"Yuccch," Chris said, "we'd better take lots of Tylenol with us."

We laughed. Then Chris became serious again. "Mom, Sarge isn't going to go to Australia with us."

"What?"

"I can't say anything," Chris said.

"You can't say anything about what?"

"Mom, I'll tell you if you promise you don't say anything to her."

"I promise," I said.

Chris began: "Remember the day me and Sarge and Rob went hiking in the canyon?"

"Yeah," I said, "the day Auntie Sylvie and I went sightseeing in Beverly Hills?"

"On the way home, I heard Sarge and Rob talking. They thought I was sleeping in the back of the Jeep. Rob said that he wanted her to come out and live with him right away. Sarge said that she couldn't come until summer. Then she started crying. She said that it made her real sad to leave us," Chris said, now crying.

I pulled Chris toward me. He pasted his small body against mine. We held each other, drawing strength.

"Honey," I said, "it's going to be just fine."

"Mom," Chris said, reading my eyes, "I knew it would make you sad, too. First Dad—now Margaret."

"It makes me very sad," I said.

As I was groping for comforting words, Chris, leaps and bounds ahead of me, said, "Yeah, but it'll make Sarge real happy. Mom, you should see the two of them together. They really love each other."

"Did you see them holding hands when they thought we weren't around?" I asked Chris.

"Yeah," Chris said, "and I even saw Rob *kiss* Sarge."

"You little devil," I said, roughing him up.

It had been a long time since we just rolled on the floor, playing.

That night, Chris and I decided that we wouldn't let on that we knew anything. We'd wait until Margaret broke the news. We also decided that we'd sleep in our sleeping bags around the fire to mark a new beginning. After all, as Chris said, "Mom, if we're going to the Outback, *you're* going to need to toughen up."

CHAPTER 18

BETWEEN NEW YEAR'S and Valentine's Day my rambling cottage turned into a rowdy halfway house. On February 1, Mrs. Hollenbeck announced that after twelve years in the nanny business she was closing up shop.

"The competition has killed me!" she said the afternoon she called to ask me a "little" favor. "In the last two years four agencies have opened up," Mrs. Hollenbeck whined. "They've scooped up all the best girls."

"I'm sorry to hear that," I said, my mind flashing to Mrs. Kibble. She sent us a Christmas card: "Dear Fullers: Merry Christmas and Happy New Year." Actually I didn't know what it said. It had been written in mirror image. It was Margaret who held it up in front of a mirror to decipher the holiday message.

Mrs. Hollenbeck said: "The last girl I placed, hit a parked car going eighty miles an hour."

"I think I heard about her," I said, recalling the Saga of Sven the Saab dealer.

"Oh, that sex-starved Swede!" Mrs. Hollenbeck said. "He tried to climb in bed with her *every* night. No wonder the poor girl . . ."

"So, what can I do for you?" I asked.

"I have the most charming young girl from . . ."

"Nebraska," I cut in.

"From Finland," Mrs. Hollenbeck corrected. "She's waiting to be placed with a family in New York. She is a dream come true."

"And her parents are farmers?" I interjected.

Mrs. Hollenbeck put down the phone, ruffled through papers, scolded her Pekinese for lifting his leg, and said, "They have a goat farm outside Helsinki."

Why did I bother to ask?

"Mrs. Hollenbeck," I said, "are you asking if I'll take her in?"

"It would just be for one day, possible two."

Time out. Where did I hear those words before?

"But I already have Margaret," I said.

"Anna has no place to go," Mrs. Hollenbeck said, practically choking back tears.

Her next words were predictable.

"It would be very good for your son to be exposed to a second language," she said. "Christopher can feel important by helping Anna learn English."

Right, I thought. Maybe I should remind Mrs. Hollenbeck of Danka. Danka was Nanny Number Thirteen—five nannies before Margaret. Danka arrived with a Danish attitude. Although she didn't speak *one* word of English, she made it quite clear that she didn't warm to seven-year-old boys. When Danka left—three weeks later—she was fluent—in expletives.

Chris taught Danka that "shoes" were called "shits," "fork" was "fuck," and "face" was "fart."

Danka's parting words to us were: "Thank you for letting Danka stay in your crappy pisshole. Madame has made Danka a very happy bitch."

"But, Mrs. Hollenbeck," I pleaded, "why can't Anna stay with you?"

"I'm about to tell you," she scolded. "My mother is quite ill. I'm leaving for Boston as soon as I hang up."

Why did I have a hard time believing this? Why did I agree to take her in? Why did it take me two weeks to realize that Anna cleaned out the liquor cabinet the way the Finns cleaned out the Lapps?

Had Margaret not been bitten by the love bug, she would

have certainly detected that the Finnish farmer's daughter was el stinko from noon on.

"Anna," I said, surprising her in the kitchen, "you've been drinking."

"Skoal!" she said, collapsing onto the floor.

Anna was dead weight. She couldn't answer even if she wanted to. I went to the liquor cabinet. The vodka bottle was empty.

"The rest are filled with tap water, ma'am," Margaret said, giving the sniff test.

Anna denied having tampered with the liquor bottles. The leggy Finn also denied having a fling with a chap called Salvatore (Fat Cat) Bonavedio. A cigar-chomping cousin to a boss of a crime family in the city.

"You know, Margaret," I said, the evening Anna packed her bags and slid into Salvatore's Lincoln Town Car, "this is the *second* time in two years that the FBI's been here."

Margaret looked up from writing Rob and smiled, "I wonder how Mrs. Kibble's doing?"

"Chris got a Valentine's Day card," I said.

"Mirror image?" Margaret asked, dryly.

"No," I said. "Pig Latin."

Margaret roared. She thought I was joking until I showed her the bright red hand-made card with the paper doily heart that read: "Appy Hay Alentines Vay Ay Day."

"Ma'am," Margaret said, "maybe one day you'll write about all of this."

"Maybe," I said. "I wonder what kind of ending it'll have?"

Margaret looked away. The time was right for her to break the news. I steeled myself. When she didn't say anything, I helped her: "You know, Margaret, Cruit's come a long way since you've been with us."

Margaret's eyes welled.

"Boy, when I think of those eighteen nannies that we had to go through to get you."

The room was so quiet I could hear the German shepherd at the end of the road.

"God," I said, "Chris can pratically take care of himself now."

"Excuse me, ma'am," Margaret, checking her Timex, "I promised Cruit that I'd go a few minutes early and watch basketball practice. Then we're goin' to shoot some baskets and go to McDonald's."

I guessed it wasn't the right time.

During the next month everything was more or less status quo. Chris was in the basketball championship. Margaret was coaching him. I was up to my eyeballs in books about Australia. At the end of our snow-coated road, nothing had changed much either. Janet and the kids were in Boca and Howard was in Anna—the leggy Finn.

According to Margaret (who heard it from Darlene who had heard it from Helga), Anna dumped Salvatore "Fat Cat" because he wanted her to have colossal breast implants and tabledance at Headlights—one of the family's clubs in the city. Hardly a thing for a respectable goat farmer's daughter.

I got the story that Howard bumped into Anna at the Pasta Patio while she was posting a situation-wanted notice: "Finnish gurl to whatch childs. Gud refrense. *Muss* hav weakents off."

Jesus, I thought, who would give her a reference. The Gambino family?

Although Howard couldn't offer Anna employment, he could give her perks under the table—so to speak. And since Anna had an attraction to the underworld, she was putty in his hands. But she was a Cruella de Ville in bed.

If Helga, the yodeler, fulfilled Howard's Heidi complex, Anna brought to fruition his Marquis de Sade syndrome.

When Darlene found out about Howard and Anna, and the goings-on in the Jack LaLanne room, she phoned Janet in Florida: "A fit Finn from a goat farm who fornicates?"

"Who gives a shit?" Janet said.

So Janet had come a long way.

"For the first time I feel as if I'm liberated from Howie's mishegoss," Janet said when I sat with her at the basketball championship. Jason and Chris were on the same team. At the last minute, Margaret was called in as the assistant coach.

"How'd you get to that point?" I asked Janet during halftime.

"A friend at the club wrote a book: *One Question That Can Save Your Marriage.*"

"What's the question?" I asked.

"What's it like to be married to me?"

"That's provocative," I said.

"I read it cover to cover. I gave it a lot of thought. I came to the conclusion that I haven't been exactly a picnic. You know that whole craziness about the flash cards when the kids were babies? I was doing it to fulfill some neurotic need within *me.* And the swimming lessons, and the Suzuki violin, and the S.A.T. for preschoolers. Pffff! I mean, did Plato's mother flash stone tablets in front of his infant eyes? Did Aristotle's mother toss him into the Aegean Sea to either sink or swim at the age of eight weeks? Did Einstein's mother pass along math formulas to him in utero? Did Heifetz's mother put a Stradivarius in his crib?"

Janet really had done some introspective work.

"After I finished the book, I gave it to Howie," Janet said.

"And?"

"He said that if *I* could turn him on, our marriage would work."

"Oh, Jesus!"

Janet rolled her eyes: "His way of trying to make it work was to buy me a 'fetching' peasant dress, antique lace-up boots, and a white crocheted nightcap at the consignment shop on Main Street. When I came out of the shower, it was displayed on the bed next to a curly brown wig."

Janet cheered when Jason almost scored. Then she lowered her voice and said: "I went into the bathroom and put on the Maid Marian get up. But instead of wearing the brown ringlet wig, I got out that red fright wig from Party Barn."

By this time everybody around us was looking at us to see what could possibly be so funny when our team was getting creamed.

Janet went on: "I called to Howie to turn off all the lights. Howie called back in old English: "Hear ye, hear ye, 'tis near the betwitchin' hour me dark-hair'd wench!"

"You've got to be kidding," I said, knowing full well she wasn't.

Janet continued: "I slipped in beside Lancelot. He said: 'I be askin' me virgin lass to be leavin' yer boots on.' After my thing with Danny, Howie could only 'do it' if he thought of me as a virgin."

"Brother," I said.

"I'm getting to the good part," Janet said, anxious to tell all. "He told me to 'feel his sword.' He had Reynolds Wrap around his little unit."

"That guy's a real piece of work," I said.

"You're tellin' me?"

"Then what?" I asked.

"Then I flicked on the light, and he went *bat shit* when he saw the red fright wig."

"Janet, you owe it to yourself to dump him."

"You think there're a lot of guys out there like Howard?" Janet asked as Margaret blew the whistle, ending the third quarter.

I jerked my head toward Margaret, "She's got a terrific guy."

"That's what I hear," Janet said. "Think they'll get married?"

In that instant I had a plan. "Janet," I said, "will you do me a favor?"

"Sure."

I took Janet into my confidence and told her what Chris had said to me. "I have to think of *some* way to let Margaret know that it's okay if she leaves to be with Rob . . . I've got to get it across to her that she's not going to be deserting us."

"I see what you mean," Janet said, more than willing to help.

"Here's my plan," I said. "The next time Margaret goes to your house to see Darlene make a real point of mentioning how *fantastic* Chris and I are doing. Say things like how adjusted we are. How far Chris has come. How far I've come. Things like that."

"No problem," Janet said. "In fact the girls are going out

tonight. I heard Darlene say that Margaret was going to pick her up around eight."

"Be casual," I warned.

As it turned out, Margaret never went out with Darlene that evening. She ended up taking the Knicks out for pizza to soothe the stinging loss.

Chris and Margaret got back home around eight. They rented *Top Gun* and convinced me to watch it.

"Mom," Chris said, "there's no hand-to-hand violence. Just F–14s kicking butt."

"It's a love story," Margaret added, knowing my weakness.

Halfway through the movie I asked: "Does the fighter pilot end up with the girl?"

"That would ruin the story, ma'am," Margaret said, scooping up a handful of popcorn.

Chris zonked before the end of the movie. I had to admit that it was entertaining. I even got a perverse thrill out of the air battles. Maybe Margaret would leave me her *Time/Life* War Series?

"So Tom Cruise got the girl," I said as Margaret rewound the movie.

"Yep," Margaret said, offering nothing more.

"I liked the way it ended," I said, fishing. "The fighter pilot and the girl living happily ever after.

"Yes, ma'am," Margaret muttered, lifting Chris and carrying him to bed.

The following morning we woke to a foot of snow in the driveway and a baggie of snow in the guest room.

"Mom," Chris said, swinging a plastic sandwich baggie filled with what looked like flour, "I was looking for my boots in the guest room, and I found this inside this weird shoe."

Chris held up a black pump with a stiletto heel. I immediately recognized it as Anna's. I quickly connected the pumps, to Salvatore Fat Cat, to the Lincoln Town Car, to the baggie Chris was holding. I added it all up: Cocaine.

"Chris," I demanded, "put that down this instant! Go wash your hands!"

Then I hollered: "Margaret!"

"Sarge is trying to get the Mustang started," Chris said looking at me as if I were out of my mind for coming unglued over a little bag of white stuff.

"That's coke all right," Margaret said with no uncertainty.

"Are you *sure*?" I asked.

Margaret was sure.

"My God, what are we going to do?" I said.

"Call the authorities," Margaret said about as collected as I. "Ma'am, this much coke has a street value of maybe a half a million."

"Jesus!" I shrieked. "Don't touch it!."

Margaret picked up the phone.

"Who are you calling?" I panicked.

"The police," Margaret said. Her hand was shaking. She dropped the phone.

"Hang it up," I ordered. "Where's Chris?"

"In his room," Margaret said. "Constructing a Messerschmitt Bf-110G with Leggos."

"Margaret, make sure he stays there. We have to plan our next move."

"Yes, ma'am," Margaret said in collusion.

Margaret and I sat silent for what seemed like hours, but it was only minutes.

"Margaret," I said, stealing a peek out the window, "the three of us have our fingerprints on that bag."

Margaret nodded.

"How can we prove that it's not ours?" I asked.

"Because if it's ours," Margaret said, "Why would we be callin' the police?"

"Good question," I said. "But I just can't shake this sinking feeling that we're going to be under suspicion."

Margaret thought for a long while: "There's always that chance, ma'am."

"Margaret, we've got to get rid of it." I heard a loud rumbling noise outside and jumped.

"It's only a snowplow," Margaret said, peering out from behind the shutters.

"We're acting suspicious," I said.

"I know that, ma'am."

"Let's get rid of it on our own," I said.

"How do you propose to do that?"

"We'll dump it down the toilet," I said, thinking back to when I was a teenager. I threw a watebasket full of cigarette butts down the toilet. The toilet backed up, and I was grounded.

"Margaret," I said, "do you know what happens when cocaine mixes with water?"

"Could explode, ma'am," Margaret said, staring at the bulging baggie as if it were a time bomb ready to go off.

"What if we bury it?"

"Ground's frozen," Margaret said.

"Let's go out for a little ride," I said, suddenly sounding like Fat Cat.

"Yes, ma'am."

"But, first," I said, "take Chris over to Jason's. Tell Janet we've got to go shopping. Make up whatever you want."

"Aye, aye, sir."

By the time Margaret slid her Mustang back into our unplowed driveway, Howard was on the phone.

"Are you two girls okay?" he asked, more than willing to render services.

"Of course we're okay," I said, I had my car keys in one hand and the baggie in the other.

"Chris seems concerned that there's a problem," Howard said, as if his own life shouldn't keep him busy enough.

"No problem, Howard," I said. Then I thought to ask him where Anna was.

"Anna?" he said.

I guessed that making buck-tooth impressions with alginate for so many years had caused memory loss.

"The Finnish nanny," I reminded. I bit my tongue from saying Darlene's line: The fit Finn from a goat farm who . . .

"Fat Cat's old lady," I said.

"Oh, her," he suddenly recalled.

"Howard, I have to know where she is."

"How would I know?" he said, bewildered.

He pushed me far enough. "Because you treated her to clear braces? Doesn't she have to come in twice a month to get *tightened*? Professional courtesy?"

Howard became defensive. "She's paying me so much every month."

"I don't doubt that, Howard," I said.

"Liz," he said, indignant, "you're out of line. Darlene's been spreading rumors that could destroy my practice."

Finally I said, "Howard, your friend Anna with the clear braces and neon elastics has us in deep shit!"

I told him about the cocaine inside the black stiletto and that Margaret and I—and even little *Chris*—could take the rap.

There was dead silence on the other end.

"Howard," I said, "are you there?"

"My brother-in-law's with the narcotics squad in the city," he volunteered. "I'll turn it over to him."

All during this conversation, Margaret had been listening on the extension.

"You've got five minutes to get your butt over here," Margaret said, slamming the phone down.

In four minutes Howard rang the doorbell. He was wearing a fur hat like Boris Yeltsin, and he was carrying a Ghost Busters lunch box.

"Where's the stuff?" he choked. His eyes were shifting from side to side. His hands were trembling.

"Margaret," I said, "get the bag."

Margaret had wiped our fingerprints off with alcohol. Using tongs she picked up the sandwich baggie with the twist tie from the kitchen counter and passed it to Howard. No words were exchanged between them. I did, however, notice Howard checking out Margaret's behind as she turned.

"Keep us out of this Howard," I demanded.

"Maggot, if you implicate us," Margaret said making a fist, "it's the five-knuckle-refresher-course."

Before Howard took the bag, he put on a pair of kiddy stretch gloves with suspender clips dangling. Then he gingerly placed the baggie inside a cardboard box that said: PLASTER IMPRESSIONS.

"And you can give these to your girlfriend, too," Margaret said, tossing him the stilettos.

"I don't know where she is," he said, as nervous as a cat.

"Tell that to somebody who believes you," Margaret snapped.

"I'm driving into the city now," he said, stepping into a snowdrift. "I'll make contact with you later in the day."

With those words Howard got into his four-wheel-drive Cherokee and was off.

At five o'clock the phone rang. It was Howard. Margaret grabbed one phone, I grabbed the other.

"Am I speaking to Lucy or Ethel?" he crowed.

Not amused, I said, "What did you find out?"

"Girls, your 'cocaine' is sold in drugstores under the generic label of 'foot powder'!"

Margaret and I had the same response. We hung up on him. Then we went limp with laughter.

Later I said to Margaret, "Why were you so certain it was cocaine?"

"Movies, ma'am."

It suddenly occurred to me to check out the liquor cabinet.

"Margaret," I said, "these liquor bottles aren't filled with tap water."

"They're not?" Margaret said, inspecting them again for color and odor.

"Hmmmmm," Margaret said. "Guess I was wrong."

"How'd you make that mistake?" I asked.

"Old Humphrey Bogart movie, ma'am."

Once again we fell to the floor like two goofy kids.

CHAPTER 19

ON APRIL FIRST, I came down to the kitchen to find Margaret and Christopher at the breakfast table squabbling.

"Sarge," Chris screeched, "I hear an HH–53H overhead!"

Margaret ran to the side door and looked to the sky. "Negatory!" she barked.

"April Fool's!" Chris squealed with delight.

"Cruit," Margaret snapped, "you've got ten minutes to chow down and police the yard."

"I thought we were going to the rifle range?"

"Shit-canned," she said, giving no explanation.

"But you promised," Chris whined.

"That was before," Margaret said, disgruntled over something.

Chris stormed off. "Sarge, you've been mean to me all week." He muttered under his breath: "Jar-head." That was slang for Marine.

"Cup of joe, ma'am?" Margaret said, reaching for the coffee pot.

"Please," I said, expecting to hear what the altercation was all about.

We ate our breakfast in silence. Apparently Margaret felt it was just between her and Chris. She was more involved in making a roster of duties for the following week.

"More joe?" Margaret asked, pouring herself a cup.

"No, thanks," I said, flipping through *Harper's Bazaar*.

"Hey, Margaret, listen to your horoscope. It says: 'You're especially sensitive this month and blow minor problems out of proportion.'"

I looked up at her. Her green eyes bulged. I went on: "'Don't let temporary frustrations prevent you from working toward your dream. Around the fourth or fifth an emotional attachment requires some soul-searching. Mars, Venus and Mercury in Virgo indicate adjustments have to be made in your personal life.'"

Margaret snorted. "I think you should be readin' that to Janet from another planet, ma'am."

"Should I go on?" I asked the skeptic.

Margaret shrugged her shoulders. I continued: "'Look to friends for support on a major decision you've made recently concerning switching careers. An underlying fear . . .'"

"Thank you, ma'am," Margaret said, cutting me off. "I've heard enough of that drivel."

"I don't have much faith in astrology either," I said. But then I thought about the uncanny reading I'd had ten years earlier in India. I began to tell Margaret about it. She appeared to be only half-listening, until I got to the astrologer's prediction that in two years I would have a son.

"How much after that time was Cruit born?" Margaret wanted to know.

"Twenty-three months and three days," I said.

Margaret started up the dishwasher and reluctantly said, "There *might* be somethin' to it." She wiped down the refrigerator door and added. "But it would take more than that to convince me that our destiny is fixed in the stars."

"Well, can you relate to anything I just read in your horoscope this month?" I asked.

"It was all very general, ma'am."

I decided to drop it.

"So what do you and Chris have planned for today?"

Margaret went to the calendar. "Rifle practice at 1300. But it's canceled."

"That's too bad," I said. "Christopher's been talking about it all week."

For the first time Margaret turned on me. *Me,* the X.O., whom she practically saluted each time we passed.

"Ma'am, it's near impossible to run this camp with conflicting forces!"

"Are you refering to me?"

"Yes, ma'am," Margaret said with no hesitation.

"Margaret, I just asked a simple question."

"Ma'am, if I'm goin' to stay at this duty station, Cruit will need to shape up or ship out."

"Has he been misbehaving?" I asked.

"Inconsistent in takin' responsibility, ma'am."

"But he's only nine."

"He wants to go to the Academy."

"That's ten years away," I said. "God, when I was his age I wanted to be a nun. And when I was thirteen I was wearing an ankle bracelet and lipstick."

From the expression on Margaret's face, I shouldn't have shared that. I backpedaled, "But knowing Chris, he'll probably end up at the Academy."

"Basic training starts right now," Margaret said. "I'm not goin' be around forever."

"How long *are* you going to be around, Margaret?"

Margaret's eyes clouded. So did mine. We just looked at each other, sparing words that couldn't possibly communicate the depth of emotion.

"Sometimes words get in the way," I said.

"Yes, ma'am," Margaret whispered.

"It's time for you to fly, Margaret," I said, holding back the Great Salt Lake. "You and Rob have a whole life. He needs you, Margaret. I mean, who's going to help him with that windmill and the log cabin? And he's got his heart set on having a kid."

"Thank you, ma'am." A tear rolled down Margaret's smiling cheek.

Then in Marine tradition, she pulled herself together. Fumbling, she plucked up the *Harper's Bazaar,* flipped to the horoscope page and read Chris's sign. "Holy Fubar," she said, "Mars, Venus and Mercury give Cruit the go-ahead for risk-takin' between the first and third."

"That's now," I said.

"Guess we'll go to the rifle range after all."

No sooner did Margaret get those words out than Chris flung open the door: "Mom, Sarge, guess what?"

"You spotted an HH–53H overhead while you were policin' the yard?" Margaret said, winking at me.

"Not even close!" he said, jumping up and down. "Darlene's going to be on 'Jeopardy!'"

"April Fool's," Margaret said.

"I promise!" Chris begged. "It's the *truth*."

Just then Jason burst through the back door. Darlene was at his heels. She was waving a letter to confirm the story.

Margaret wasn't the only one who had a dream come true.

CHAPTER 20

"MARGARET," I said, "have you ever fantasized about what it would be like to meet the person you've spent your life idolizing?"

Margaret took but a moment to respond. "Many times."

"Who would it be?" I asked.

"General Patton, ma'am."

"And what if one day General Patton came to your house for dinner? And the next day moved in? With a tank full of his war memorabilia? And then the four-star general proceeded to take over your household? 'Margaret,' he'd order, 'we're out of Maalox and toilet paper,' or 'Margaret, did I ever tell you how I got the worse case of bunions on my sweep through Germany?'"

Margaret burst out laughing. "That's a hard one to imagine, ma'am." Then with Margaret's usual directness she asked: "What's your point."

"Margaret, I'm going to write a one-woman show on how *my* favorite movie star, Bette Davis, came here for dinner, and the very next day moved in with eighteen pieces of Mark Cross luggage, and proceeded to take command of our lives. I mean there I was every morning sitting at the breakfast table with The Legend, listening to her deliver her drop-dead lines."

Margaret flipped a couple of eggs and asked, "What made you decide to write about it now?"

"This may sound awfully silly," I said, "but I decided the

day Darlene came over and told us she was going to be on "Jeopardy!"

Margaret did a double take. "Not sure I'm readin' you."

"You see, Margaret, Darlene's dream was to be a contestant on the game show, and I thought: What is *my* dream? That same night, it came to me: To actually perform in a show *I've* written."

"Hope you include the part about Sun Lee not wantin' to eat the movie star's baked beans," Margaret said, chuckling to herself.

Later in the week Margaret came to my office. "Hate to disturb you in the middle of your work hours, but I got a little somethin' here I think you'll be interested in."

"Shoot," I said, expecting to hear about Rob and their future plans, which really weren't that far in the future. Margaret was planning on leaving at the end of the summer. I tried to convince her to leave in June, but she wouldn't hear of it. She and Chris had too many things planned.

Margaret read: "Your horoscope for June says: 'Saturn in your sign signifies it's time for you to follow your dream. By the tenth a writing or acting project could take off. Stick to your agenda.'" Margaret looked up from the magazine as if she almost believed in what she read. Then she got a mischievous grin and continued: "'At mid-month sensitive Virgo meets flexible Aquarius.'"

The flexible Aquarius never materialized. What did materialize was a crazed Capricorn who had one goal in life: To eliminate his ex-wife. "I could hire a woodchipper," the pharmaceutical sales rep said with a maniacal laugh that attracted the attention of half the restaurant.

"Or you could take her out on the Sound," I said, joking along.

He became dead serious. "How far out?"

"Maybe a mile," I said, suddenly uncomfortable with his intensity.

"After her latest liposuction, she'd probably float to the top," he said with a frustrated look.

"Cement shoes," I said, forcing a laugh.

He shifted his eyes, which were the size, shape and color of Swanson's early peas. Then he lowered his voice and said, "There's no such thing as cement shoes."

"Thom McAn," I said, checking my watch. "Boy, I didn't realize how late it was getting.

He slapped down his Visa and asked: "But how would I ever get the bitch on the boat?"

This guy was a shrimp short of a cocktail.

"Tell her you want to discuss increase in alimony."

"Brilliant," he said, wild-eyed.

Margaret was waiting up when I got home. "Don't even ask how it went," I said, as she clicked off the TV. Over tea, I proceeded to give her a blow-by-blow account of the whole evening. Beginning with when he picked me up and said, visibly disappointed, "You look much taller in that photo in the paper,"—to when he dropped me off—"So maybe during the week I can bring over a few samples of our new product that creams away facial hair?"

"You gotta kiss a lot of frogs," Margaret said, borrowing my words.

"You know what," I said, "I'm not even discouraged. I just feel lucky."

"That clown should be with Mrs. Kibble shufflin' around in paper slippers, ma'am."

"Margaret, what I'm about to say might sound trite, but I like my life just the way it is."

"I know that," she said.

"Can you see it?"

"Yes, ma'am. You haven't been talkin' about that cockamamie idea of you and Cruit goin' to the Outback."

"That wasn't a cockamamie idea."

Margaret went to the bookshelf and came back with a *National Geographic*. She pointed out insects the size of a small dog, man-eating crocodiles, rattlesnakes, kangaroos who can kick the guts out of you, and sweet koala bears who can turn your face into steak tartare. She even went so far as to circle the part about how Australia had started out as a penal colony.

"I suppose you showed that to Chris?"

Margaret didn't answer.

"Well, our Outback plans are on hold until I finish writing this show."

"Accordin' to your July horoscope, you'll be done at the end of the month," Margaret said. She now only half-poked fun at the stars.

The stars were right. At the end of July I sent the show to my agent. Two weeks later, I received a telephone call from a three-time Tony-winning producer, Lester Osterman.

"Elizabeth," said the voice on the other end of the line, "I just read your one-woman show."

"Yes," I said, numb.

"I think it can go somewhere," he said.

"My show?" I said, unprepared, unbelieving, unglued.

"*Me and Jezebel*," he said, as if double-checking to see if he had the right person on the line.

"Cool," I said, sounding more like my son than a budding playwright talking to a famous producer.

"Who do you see playing you?" he asked.

I hesitated. "Me."

"You?"

"Well," I apologized, "I really feel as if I'm the only one who can do it because it happened to me."

"But you're not an actress."

"I know, but I still feel as if I'm supposed to do it."

There was silence.

"But I don't necessarily have to do it."

"Let's have lunch," he said.

CHAPTER 21

On august 18, two weeks before Margaret was scheduled to leave, I gave my first performance of *Me and Jezebel* at the Westport Arts Center. I had convinced Lester Osterman to give me a chance. If it was a total bust, there was always the Outback.

It was a full house. The reaction was more than any of us had expected. In fact it was so positive, the arts center asked if I'd do six performances the following month as a benefit. Whether it ever went any further than Westport, Connecticut, didn't matter. I felt as cocky as Darlene when she answered the question on "Jeopardy!" that won her $2,000 and the ability to go on to the Daily Double.

Immediately following the show was a question-and-answer period. The audience was teeming with curiosity: "Why didn't John just toss Bette out? Did she ever pay you for all those overseas calls? What about the groceries? Did she really color with Chris? Why did she hate Crawford so? Did Crawford really have bosoms of three different sizes? Exactly how did Ms. Davis's spinning cigarette set your living-room draperies on fire?"

But the question that registered with the most poignancy was: "Mrs. Fuller, what's your next project?"

I took a deep breath and blurted, "I'm going to write about three very special people."

I looked into the front row to where Margaret was sitting with Chris sound asleep on her shoulder. "Two are here tonight," I said, making eye contact with Margaret. "And the other is with me always."

That same night, Margaret fixed us our customary tea and asked, "So how's the story goin' to start, ma'am?"

"That's a tough one," I said. "Got any ideas?"

Margaret swirled honey into the Twinings, played with the tea bag and said, "How 'bout beginnin' the book with me knockin' on your front door? Something like: 'Sergeant Margaret Stone reportin' for duty, ma'am.'"

"Margaret," I said, "that's nothing short of brilliant!"

"It is?" she said, grinning.

"It says it all. Nothing flowery. No fat. Simple. Direct. I love it. Tomorrow I begin with those words as my opening sentence," I said, writing her words on a Bounty paper towel.

Margaret sipped her tea and with the sudden confidence of a Stephen King said, "Now, your second sentence should grab the reader. It should be a vivid portrayal of the dangers posed to families by incompetent nannies." Margaret grabbed a Bounty and pencil and began to write: "Here's your second sentence: 'Sergeant Margaret Stone was no ordinary . . .'"

"Margaret," I said, "I'll keep my hands off your Messerschmitt Bf 110G balsa model, if you keep your hands off my book."

"Yes, ma'am," she said joining me in a good laugh.

But before we turned off the lights, I asked Margaret, "If you should come up with an *ending* to this story, let me know."

"I'll sleep on it, ma'am," she said, bolting the door.

Ever since Margaret thought she saw Fat Cat's Town Car cruising up and down our sleepy tree-lined road searching for Anna, we kept the doors double-bolted.

Several days later, Margaret came down to the breakfast table. With puffy eyes she handed me a sheet of notebook paper.

"The ending of your book, ma'am."

It was a note Chris had written to Margaret and left on her dresser.

"Sarge," Chris printed, "you were here when we needed you, and now it's time for you to change duty stations. Don't worry, I'll take good care of Mom. I wish you fair weather and following winds.

I'll always love you, Sarge. Cruit."

THE TEN COMMANDMENTS
FOR LIVING WITH
NANNIES

IN THIS BOOK, I have shared with you some of our family's most outrageous experiences with nannies who helped care for my son Christopher, now age ten. Mercifully, with the passage of time, we can now laugh about some of the wild and zany characters who crossed our threshold. Perhaps some of our former nannies are dining out on hilarious stories about us.

Yet bringing a stranger into your home to help care for your children is no joke. In fact, it can be a harrowing and stressful experience for any household. Would you stop your shiny new BMW for a hitchhiker, hop out and offer to let him drive? Of course not. Yet you trust a nanny to care for something far more precious—your little shnookums, your special little guy, your princess, your progeny.

At the same time, the right nanny can become an extension of your family and enrich the quality of life in your home. If the match between nanny and family clicks, the experience can be growth-enhancing for children and parents alike, as well as for the nanny.

To help maximize the chances for success, I offer Liz Fuller's *Ten Commandments for Living with Nannies.*

I. THOU SHALT ASK BEAUCOUP QUESTIONS

Your first chance to get a feel for your prospective nanny is the interview. Pepper her with questions. The more you can learn, the better.

Start informally. What are your hobbies? Casually observe her ankles for telltale bungee burns. Then check her wrists for handcuff scrapes. Such nannies are too active. But you also don't want her to be too dreamy and laid back. Do you like sports? This is an important question if your children don't particularly enjoy spending their days meditating to flute music.

How long a commitment can you make to our family? If you notice a job application for the French Foreign Legion sticking out of her Guatemalan knapsack, you might want to end the interview.

Do you have a police record? Most likely she will respond with a giggle, roll her eyes and say, "Pfffff." Regardless of the precious Laura Ashley interview frock and pink ballet slippers, make a note to phone her hometown police and see if she has a record.

Have you ever received a traffic violation? How many? Have you ever been involved in an auto accident? If so, please describe. Ask to see her driver's license. One nanny I interviewed actually showed me a photo I.D. to Gold's Gym. I later learned that her license had been suspended for driving naked with five guys and a six-pack.

To glean how she might relate to your family, try to find out what kind of relationship she had with her own parents. Of course, no nanny is likely to explode in unchecked rage and blurt out, "Like, my parents need a life!" You can ask, gently: Are your parents supportive of your decision to become a nanny? Have you ever been separated from your family for any length of time? Did you get homesick?

Lifestyle questions are a must.

Do you like to stay up late? How late? Are you an early riser? How early? *IMPORTANT!* After getting these answers, apply the Fuller Time/ Phase Factor, which reliably tells you the actual times she goes to bed and gets up. To do this, simply add four hours to the times provided.

Do you watch a lot of television? What are your favorite shows? If you get a nonstop recitation of the comings and going of five or more soap operas, it's possible that your child's finger-painting class at the Y will be scratched for "The Young and the Restless."

What is your favorite movie? If she chuckles and answers, *Honey, I Ditched the Kids,* that's a bad sign.

Do you believe children should be disciplined? She probably won't say, "I've always found that the Five-Knuckle-Refresher-Course keeps them in line." But you *can* ask how she herself was disciplined. Psychologists say a child who was hit may become an adult who hits.

Do you enjoy preparing meals? Do you think Cheez Whiz is one of the major food groups?

Do you smoke, drink, or take drugs? Again, don't expect to hear, "All *right!* You know where I can score some realllly good weed?" But she might volunteer information about legal drugs. If she takes a prescription drug to suppress multiple personalities, it could be a problem if the medication wears off while she's driving Benjamin to preschool.

Will she be tolerant of your family's religious beliefs? Fundamentalists of many denominations can be censorious, especially toward social drinking. Let's say you've invited your minister over for dinner. It can ruin the mood if your nanny bursts into the dining room, slaps the glass from his hands and tearfully lectures him on damnation through spirits.

Of course, ask the customary: Why do you want to be a nanny? Have you ever worked as a nanny before? If so, please tell us about your experiences. What did she like about the job? What did she dislike?

Elizabeth Fuller

II. THOU SHALT FIND OUT HOW SHE THINKS

Sometimes I conclude the interview by asking an offbeat question, just to see how the nanny thinks.

What would you do if you had a day off, and could do anything in the world you wanted? I look for creative, thoughtful responses that suggest a well-adjusted, people-oriented individual. I take note of unsociable answers like, "Stay in my room with the damn door shut and play Dungeons and Dragons!"

It's perfectly all right to ask how she would handle a wide range of situations that are likely to occur during the course of her tenure. How would she react if my child whacked another child in the schnoz? Or if my child had a fever and I wasn't reachable? To get some objective distance, try making up hypothetical situations.

What would she do if:

—Tiffany wakes up terrified and convinced that Freddy Krueger is in the closet?

—Zachary inhales a plastic dinosaur egg he excavated from an early-achievement kit?

—Britanny is approached in the grocery store by a chatty stranger who looks like Pee-Wee Herman?

—Cute little Ashley tells you that she hates you, your ears look like Ronzoni shells, your acne is getting worse, your body looks like a ride at Kiddy Land and she wishes you would go back to Finland/Denmark/Iowa/Nebraska. (You can count on this happening!)

—Noah insists on zoning out in front of Nintendo all day? (If the child is a boy over five, you can also take this one to the bank.)

III. THOU SHALT ASK BUT ALSO OBSERVE

While talking to your prospective nanny, also take time to size up what kind of person she seems to be. Gut feelings or "vibes" often provide the most honest answers.

Does she appear to be overly sensitive? If she's a frail bundle of nerves, keep in mind that most children will at times be as rude and cruel as little versions of Don Rickles.

Is she compassionate, or does talking to her make you feel as if you're both trapped in an episode of "Married with Children"?

If your candidate is a serious one, invest in a nice long chat with her. Get the other family members to join in. Would you be comfortable with this person living under your roof, day after day? Is she a soothing presence, or does her voice remind you of fingernails scraping along a chalkboard?

Oh, yes, table manners. Invite her to join you for a family dinner. She's unlikely to chug milk from the carton, or wrap her lips around the kitchen faucet that first evening, but make a note of it if she slurps, burps and scoops food with her fingers like a Fisher-Price steam shovel. It's also bad if she responds to questions at the dinner table by shouting "Shuddup, I'm eating," as she smushes the corn and mashed potatoes back into her mouth.

Use of the English language. Does she say: "Ahh-ma-Gawd-I-am-soooo-grossed-out," while attempting to feed your drooling and puking infant? If so, you might want to look for a foreign-speaking nanny. Her attitude will be the same, but at least you won't know what she's saying.

Ask her to take your car for a spin, with you as the passenger. Buckle up. Does she blend eye shadow in the rearview mirror while exiting highway ramps? Does she cast glances in all directions, smiling at boys in sports cars while revving the engine? Does her head whirl around like the girl in *The Exorcist*?

If a candidate seems too good to be true and you want further proof, concoct a little experiment to see how she behaves under everyday nanny conditions. For example, leave her alone for fifteen minutes in a room with (a) your baby, (b) a television, (c) scattered Leggos and (d) four giant boxes of Oreos and Mallomars.

Give no instructions.

Come back into the room. Did you trip over Leggos? Was

the baby hyperventilating? Was the TV on full blast? Were the cookies gone? If so, that's about par for the course. But if the would-be nanny has scarfed all the cookies and run to the bathroom to "call Earl" on the "Big Phone," look further into her eating habits.

By the way, if you suspect a severe eating disorder, or any other major personal problem, it is reasonable for you to arrange to chat with her family and ask straightforward questions. A nanny is not just an employee. She is under your roof, and technically under your care.

If you think you've found your perfect nanny, you might want to ask if she'd like to work for a few days to see how you all get along. A trial run is good for her, as well as for you. During that time, closely observe:

—Does she appear patient?

—Is she a self-starter? (What you don't need is a nanny flouncing around and whining: "I'm bored. There's nothing to do around this dump." You'll get enough of that behavior from your own children in a few years.)

—Does she empathize with the kids? How does she respond when little Chloe or Joshua runs crying to her with a scraped knee? Does she cuddle the child or is her attitude, "Like, tell it to someone who cares!"

And, of course, check all of her references.

Do not rely on employment agencies.

IV. THOU SHALT AGREE ON ALL FINANCIAL ARRANGEMENTS

The time to nail down all of the terms of the nanny's employment is right at the beginning. Her pay and the duration of service are only part of the picture. Just about every aspect of her life in your home is fodder for future discussion, and possibly debate, about who does what.

Many situations will come up regarding her duties that you never thought about before she disembarked from KLM Flight

202, all smiles and suitcase held together with a bumper sticker reading, *Future Virgin*. Within hours you'll suddenly wonder, is helping out with the laundry part of the job? Oh-oh, how about cooking? Is "Thou Shalt Not Do Windows" on the nanny's own list of Ten Commandments?

If you ask the nanny to stay home with the kids on her night off, does she get overtime? How much?

If she drives your car to Buffalo to see "Ed," a prison pen-pal she made while a schoolgirl in Finland, who pays for the gas? You? The nanny? Certainly not Ed.

Let's say your family follows a healthy food regimen, with most meals revolving around fresh produce, light on meats, fats and sugars. If her idea of a meal is lardy pork chops, fake mashed potatoes and Ring-Dings, do you supply the junk food, or is that her responsibility?

Talk about it all up front. It's going to cost you either way, but more so if you forget to ask.

V. THOU SHALT NOT GET INVOLVED IN THY NANNY'S SOCIAL LIFE

Once your nanny arrives, there are certain things you can do to improve the odds that the relationship will be mutually satisfying. For your own sanity, make it clear from the get-go that you don't want to hear the continuing saga of her social life, or that of her friends. This is difficult. You'll want to feel like a mother hen to the nineteen-year-old who has just been dumped.

For example, your nanny might say: "Like, Jimmy just stood me up for the third time," and then burst into hysterics. Or she might try to interest you in conversation about one of her nanny friends while changing the baby. "Poor Karen, she's three months late and starting to show. She's scared they're going to find out and send her back to the pig farm. What should we do?"

Note the "we."

Again, resist the temptation to give advice. Whenever she mentions her personal life, smile and act as if she's from a remote mountainside village in Tibet and you can't understand one word of what she told you. If you don't follow this advice, there's a ninety-nine percent chance you'll be spending countless hours as an unpaid, untrained, unglued analyst.

In short, resist getting snagged in "The Nanny Web."

VI. THOU SHALT NOT TAKE THY NANNY'S PHONE MESSAGES

Once you start taking an occasional message, this will quickly escalate to where part-time employment with SPRINT would be less time-consuming. In fact, avoid getting trapped into taking any messages when one of her dozens of friends phones. It is a curious fact that within days of a nanny moving in she will have made more friends than you'll ever dream of having. I have never met a nanny wallflower.

The moment your nanny steps out of the house, the phone will ring. This is guaranteed. A mumble or heavy accent on the other end will say, "Jennythere?"

The voice never identifies itself.

Your only correct response is, "No, she isn't. Good*bye.*" Click.

Warning! Do not say one more word! If you prolong the conversation—even for an instant—I guarantee this is what you'll hear next:

"Oh, hi, excellent. Tell Jenny to call me at Bob's. Take down Bob's number. Him and me are going over to Cary's house. Take down Cary's number. Oh, yeah, here's the number for Bob's father's car phone. Cary might be on her beeper. I'll call you back with that number, okay? We'll be at Cary's for twenty minutes, after that she can like get us in the bar at the Pasta Patio. I've been having trouble starting my car, so if . . ."

When you find yourself on the receiving end of this kind of

monologue, your only hope is to make hissing, staticlike sounds back into the phone, and shout "Hello, hello," as if there is interference on the line.

Then quickly hang up.

VII. THOU SHALT SET STRICT GUIDELINES CONCERNING BOYFRIENDS

Think about this: Would it bother you if you found Al's earring under your pillow when you and your husband return from a weekend away?

Would it grate if Al walks out of the shower with a towel wrapped around his waist and says: "Yo, mama, we're out of cream and mayo."

Do you want three-year-old Kristyn riding shotgun in Sean's black Trans Am? What about eating Cheez Doodles out of the vending machine at Speedy Auto Body while waiting for Sean to lube his last car of the day?

Does the sight of *Cosmopolitan* Magazine flipped open on your nanny's bed to "When Too Much Sex Is Not Enough" concern you as you're packing for your high-school reunion in Toledo?

You're going out for the evening and you send Bibby to Stop-n-Shop for boneless chicken breasts and she returns with a frozen pizza and a box of Today Sponges. Do you suddenly feel like canceling your dinner plans?

If you can answer yes to any of the above—spell out the guidelines *before* she moves in. This will prevent conflict later on. Of course, your guidelines concerning boyfriends and sex are a matter of individual taste and values in your household. What Melanie does in the back seat of her boyfriend's Eagle is *her* business. What she does under your roof is *your* business.

Elizabeth Fuller

VIII. THOU SHALT NOT COVET THY NEIGHBOR'S NANNY

See Chapter 3.

IX. THOU SHALT NOT ALLOW HUSBAND TO INTERVIEW NANNY

His opinion simply doesn't count.
And last, but not least:

X. THOU SHALT NOT REJECT OUT OF HAND THE NANNY WHO SHOWS UP ON YOUR DOORSTEP IN MARINE FATIGUES.